HOMESCHOOL ADVENTURES

LEARNING THROUGH THE POWER OF FIELD TRIPS

MELISSA CALAPP

D1512198

Dedicated to my homeschools friends who have lead me on more adventures than I can count, helping my children and I to see the world with fresh eyes.

LIVE
LEARN
WORK AT HOME

PART I

When Learning Meets Adventure

1

A DIFFERENT WAY TO LEARN

*"Firsthand experiences are crucial to learning new
concepts as well as positioning the learner for future
educational experiences."* John Dewey[1]

There are many pieces of this puzzle we call homeschooling and many ways to arrange them. For the last nineteen years I've been finding and adding pieces to our puzzle, not always understanding what the final picture would be but getting beautiful glimpses along the way. About three years ago, I began to understand the beauty and strength to the piece we call field trips, or excursions. I'm going to blatantly try to convince you, dear reader, that these adventures are worth adding to your final picture, whatever that looks like.

I started like many young moms, taking my kids on infrequent trips. We went to all the traditional places like the zoo, museums. We learned many things and we had a lot of fun on these haphazard, occasional excursions. Somewhere in the back of my mind I knew we could and probably should be doing a lot more of these hands-on activities, but it wasn't easy to coordinate. For me the biggest hurdle was that I am a bit of a homebody. Fortunately, my job, friends, and very social kids force me out of the house quite often.

THE ADVENTURES BEGIN

THREE YEARS AGO, I WENT TO WHAT I THOUGHT WAS A CASUAL homeschool get-together. I thought I was there to help introduce a few homeschooling families to each other and meet a few new ones. It was at a church, and our children played war in the gym, boys against girls, behind the stacks of folding chairs. I have a vague memory of balls being involved. More than one child was brought to tears, so I'm pretty sure there were balls. All of the kids know each other quite well now and look back on that day with sheepish smiles and lowered lids.

The mothers sat in a circle in some of the folding chairs, not being used for the war, and planned. At first, we planned for the group to do many different types of educational activities and we started off that way, but soon everyone was suggesting ideas for field trips and offering to take turns planning. The more field trips we went on, the longer our suggested list became. Each mom seemed to know of locations and venues that the other moms had not heard of before. So we went. Every week. For the last 160 weeks. And, no, we don't take off summers, though we took off Christmas week once.

OVERCOMING EXCUSES

AT FIRST, I TOLD THEM WE WOULDN'T MAKE IT VERY OFTEN. I TRIED to come up with all the reasons in the world not to go, and I've had a lot of reasons to not go: I have to work, I had six kids of all different ages, then I was pregnant and tired, I had a newborn, a baby with special needs, doctor appointments, and there was always my work schedule, I was emotionally drained, plus my house was a mess, and my now seven kids had their own school work to get done. However, my kids outvoted me. Did I mention I have seven? So we usually went in spite of my protests. My kids have come to expect an adventure at least once a week, and I've mostly stopped trying to come up with excuses.

Usually, I am glad I have been encouraged and prodded to go. Like this week. We visited the last rural Chinese town in America. We wandered the streets and talked to the shop owners about living in a town with less than one hundred people. Then we went further up the road to a state park along the river. My baby had fallen asleep in the car, so I stayed in the car with her for awhile. After she woke, I went to find the others over the little hill to what I was told was a beach. I came across what was actually a flat area of mud. Several of the children were playing in it, rolling in it, basking in it. Others were looking for clams. Some were picking up seaweed to add to their fort. And as I walked over the muddy bank, locating and checking on my various children, I could hear contented singing. "Newsies," had come to the city near us the month before, and though the tickets were pricey, many had gone, and the phones and other devices had been playing the songs from the musical for weeks. Now I could hear snatches of "Newsies" songs almost muttered under the breath as the children were busy with their various activities in the mud and in the water.

It made me happy from the inside out. These moments are what I want for my children. They live in a beautiful world and are enjoying it, thoroughly. They grab what they want from it and carry it with them. There are so many more benefits than this joy found in adventuring, and I'll get to many of them throughout this book. The list is long.

FINDING THE RESEARCH

AS PART OF WORKING AT A CHARTER SCHOOL THAT SUPPORTS homeschoolers, I got to lead a breakout session at a conference on field trips in February. To be prepared, and since I am a reader and a psychology major by degree, I decided I would study the research and look for the studies of the benefits of field trips. I found studies which took me on several paths as to why we remember more from episodic events-field trips- than from many other ways of learning. I found studies that described the benefits and the drawbacks of field trips and other studies that tested how they can be better for the learning process, and I don't mean getting the right answer on a test somewhere.

SHOWING OTHERS THE LEARNING

AS SOMEONE WHO COLLECTS THE REPORTS FROM HOME EDUCATORS about what they have been doing, I'll help you find and put the field trip learning into words in case you need to report it. While it may be harder to articulate, it is worth going through the effort to show that not just your book learning but your hands-on adventures in the real world contribute significantly to your child's education.

MATCHING EXCURSIONS TO YOUR EDUCATIONAL PHILOSOPHIES

WHEN I FIRST MARRIED AND HAD DECIDED TO HOMESCHOOL I SPENT about four years reading every book I could find on the different philosophies of education that homeschoolers use in an ever elusive quest to find the perfect method. After I studied I taught a course about all of the different philosophies, what sets them apart and what unites them. I also did internships in as many alternative schools as I could, so that I could get a better understanding of the Montessori approach and the Waldorf approach and other alternative methods of classroom teaching, some of which carries over into homeschools and some which does not. As I learned, I tried things from various philosophies I liked with my kids and have stuck with some and moved on to others as I've gone along. I'll share how field trips fit into many of these approaches as well.

SPECIFICS, AND WHERE TO GO

I'LL HELP WITH THE HOW'S, THE WHY'S AND THEN GIVE SOME IDEAS as to where you can go to get you started. You can also email me at livelearnworkathome@gmail.com to share your thoughts and for an article on my current research about how field trips work with and benefit students with different learning styles.

Mostly, I want this book to encourage you on your way. I also want to reassure you that education is sloppy. It is okay if your child comes away from a trip talking about something like the research cow who was walking around chomping the grass with a hole in its side, so students can actively see it's digestive process, and seems to have missed the much greater point of how to get into the research university. True story.

Just because two students walk away with vastly different understanding from a trip doesn't mean one failed. It means we all win. We win when people look at things from different angles, notice different aspects, and come together from various perspectives to solve problems and create new things. Those differences are exactly the real-world experiences which open us up. They help us develop the skills that create a better conversationalist, a better employee, and a more flexible thinking adult.

While I live and explore one location, my information and depth in this place deepen, but it offers nothing to the reader who lives in another part of the country or world. So while my examples and stories give glimpses into this place at this time. I can not give you a flag to place on your map. Instead, I offer you a window, a way of looking at the places around you, to set your personal flag from what you see. While I say this, I will also give you enough ideas to take a trip every week for five years. That should be enough to get you started.

I hope to excite you, encourage you and push you a bit to take your children out into the real world. Show them what it has to offer and be there to watch their faces and hear their thoughts when they see it.

2

LEARNING IN THE REAL WORLD

"Education should move the learner outward
physically and socially, as well as intellectually."
Salvatore Vascallero

We held a contest in our homeschool group and asked kids to prepare T-shirt designs. The designs would be put to a vote at our end of the year presentation day, and we would make matching T-shirts to wear on next years trips using the winning design. My daughter created a simple graphic with the caption that said, "Homeschoolers in the *Real* World." After the vote had come in, her design resonated with our group of adventurers and won. She got to work with a graphic artist and learn how to take her design from idea to final product. It was her own personal field trip. So now when we go in a group, we have fifteen to twenty homeschoolers in our matching light blue shirts and another fifteen to twenty who couldn't find theirs that day, because that's real too.

What is homeschooling in the real world, and more importantly, why do it? It starts with getting out of the house to use the world as part of our learning. Each trip is going to be a little different because that is the way the real world is, but when we are out, we are always learning from our experiences. We are learning what real people find important, what they do, why they do it and how they do it. We are learning what real objects look like and how they influence each other and how the objects and the environment influence people. We are finding connections and adding ideas to those we already have.

Last summer our group went on a three-day guided tour in a more northern area of California. We learned about the hydraulic mining in the 1800's as we stood overlooking the bald side of a mountain. We learned about how much water the miners used and how they had to solve the problem of where that water would go as we hiked through a drainage tunnel of solid rock for a half mile underneath a mountain. The kids learned about using water pressure and what the tools looked like as they climbed all over a water cannon. We learned how the history of this area connected to the stories we had heard from an earlier trip about how Old Sacramento had flooded so often that the town decided to bring in dirt to raise the roads ten feet. On our trip to the mountains, we learned about who did that flooding and how angry it made the farmers lower down in the valley. Wouldn't you be angry too if suddenly your newly planted field was covered in muddy water and your seeds washed away? The farmers filed a lawsuit against the miners. Not only did we learn the history but we learned there are two perspectives to every controversy. The miners felt they had every right to make their living.

When we introduce kids to the disagreements of real people in history and the untidiness of it all, it can help them understand there aren't always easy solutions. The kids start to have conversations and suggest solutions that are thoughtful and look at more than the most obvious perspective. In the end, the miners lost, but some of them still continued hydraulic mining for awhile, inventing the best message relay system up to that point. A scout would watch for law enforcement officers and would warn the miners before the officers could get to the mines, saving them from arrest.

Going on this trip and seeing it all helped the kids to understand the thought processes of the people involved. They also learned about how the calculations of gold were made when water was cheap or free, and since they have been living in a drought for the last few years, they took the next logical step and asked what would happen when the water ran out, or it got expensive. They were justified in their connections when they were told that that is exactly what happened. The water got more expensive and is now much more valuable than the gold that is remaining in the hills. It would be a losing proposition for the miners. These people and their struggles and life became real for us. We can't care about history until we realize the people involved were real.

We didn't sit down with the kids and tell them that on this trip they learned history, science, and economics. If we wanted, we could calculate break-even points on water cost versus gold cost. We could have given them an English assignment to fill out the questions to earn the Junior Ranger patches from the park ranger, which many kids chose to do on their own. We didn't need to break up the trip into subjects. Sometimes for convenience we talked about the different subjects as if they exist independently of one another, but in the real world they aren't broken up. Everything collides, and by seeing the collision, students are better able to grasp the whole picture and the effects of one action on another.

LEARNING IS CONNECTED

WHEN WE GO TO COLLEGE, WE ARE ASKED TO PICK ONE FIELD TO study, but when we are out and about, we can see that jobs in the real world aren't so tidy. Science lives within our period of history and is affected by law. It's used by people. The art we produce today is affected by science and history as many hands-on museum exhibits will show you. Sometimes I think we do a disservice to kids by breaking up everything they study into little boxes and labeling them. What we need today are people to think outside these boxes, to find the connections between the science and the history, the math and the power of language. Every aspect of life is connected to hundreds of other things and it is only in our schools do we break them apart as if we could study them in isolation.

When Lindon B. Johnson became president, he took an experience from the real world with him. As a very young man he taught school in a Mexican American community. The area and people were new to him, they had needs and ideas he had not previously thought about and he learned to care. As president he refused to forget about the Mexican Americans living in poverty in all the bills he passed, because he had lived as a young teacher with them and had seen how poor some of them were. His worldview forever changed when he spent nine months seeing something he hadn't known anything about.

GROUNDING EDUCATION

THERE ARE SOME HARD QUESTIONS WE ARE ASKING TODAY. THE MORE kids can get out and see the homeless man begging for food, a convalescent hospital in an affluent area as well as in an impoverished one, the ideas coming out of innovative schools and the trials found at others. The more they can talk to people who have succeeded and others who have not, the more they are likely to think critically when they read a headline, and to ask what else is going on here? Who else does this decision affect? What are the long-range outcomes of voting for this bill? How will that new invention really change our way of life? Did that business succeed or fail based only on the one thing the journalist seems to think is the cause? How should I vote? There are a lot of very hard questions, and many of them our kids will need to answer. If students have knowledge only from the filtered information of one source, their opinions are very likely to be incomplete and lacking substance. But if they can see the world as it is, it will lead to their own questions and discussions. Often the adults will need to step back and say "I don't have the answers, what do you think?"

BREAKING THROUGH STEREOTYPES

TO ANSWER THESE QUESTIONS, WE NEED TO BE ABLE TO SEE THINGS from more than one perspective. The real world can do this. It can expand world views and can help students see situations from other people's eyes. We went to the Golden Gate bridge once and watched all the people coming to see the icon. We heard many languages spoken and we saw many people pointing excitedly and standing for photos, which was the same thing we were doing. There was a group of monks in traditional orange clothing pointing at the bridge, speaking excitedly and taking photos. What a great lesson on how we are all so similar! And what a great way to break barriers on preconceptions. I challenge you to find a textbook that describes the life of a Buddhist monk and says "and sometimes they go on vacations to see the world's most famous structures and take selfies in front of the Golden Gate Bridge."

These sorts of things crash through our stereotypes. When we live on the surface, doing the same things, interacting with the same people, having the same conversations, we can be ruled by stereotypes and fear. Entering the world and especially our own community does the opposite. It helps us to care and appreciate. Some cultures can't be understood without understanding the dynamic relationships they have with their environment, whether that's a specific neighborhood or a natural resource. Acorns as food make little sense when we learn they aren't digestible without very careful preparation, but when standing in an oak forest, surrounded by hundreds of oak trees, they do. We need the context of the environment, not always the paragraphs on the page. Though, of course, I have few complaints about a good book. We just have to remember that books are only one piece of a good education.

BUILDING CONNECTIONS TO COMMUNITY

GOING OUT HELPS CONNECT US TO OUR COMMUNITY. IT IS inherently interesting to the child who has mastered his house and is ready to expand. The child lives in a world of end-products. Many trips can be taken in search of where these end-products began. Where does the energy in our walls come from? The water? The furniture we use? The food we eat? And even the wood of our house itself? Where do these things come from and who is involved in getting it to us?

We can ask similar questions by walking around our towns and cities. There are a wealth of things to learn in our communities. Take a walk and ask everywhere you go, could this be a field trip? Could we learn anything from the law office, the nail salon, the tutoring center, the vacuum repair shop or the lumberyard?

Getting out into the real world can also start from a subject a child is studying. For instance, a child studying economics might use a website such as http://www.jumpstart.org/reality-check.html or cut photos from magazines or list what they think a family of four needs to live. They may calculate the income they need to afford this lifestyle. This is all well and good, but not likely to leave a strong, lasting memory. If, instead of stopping there, they extend their studies by looking up the average incomes of different neighborhoods near them, walking through these neighborhoods, keeping in mind their lists of what lifestyle they think a family should have, and then comparing the real life averages of these areas with their earlier calculations, then, a lasting impression is more likely to be made, because it is real. This realness increases the brain's ability to remember, since it is attached to a concrete event.

FINDING OUR PLACE

AS WE UNDERSTAND MORE ABOUT OUR WORLD, WE LEARN THE history of it and we begin to understand where our spot in it can be. By getting out in the world, barriers are not only broken down, but opportunities students didn't know exist are brought before them. Think for a moment about how many jobs and careers are out there. Our children witness jobs in action, jobs they may have never heard of or seen before. They can also see what people do on jobs with which they are already familiar.

Local colleges are ideal for introducing students to a variety of occupations. I try to watch the calendar of our local junior college for visiting lecturers and seminars. These are designed for college students but open to anyone and often free. I took my oldest children and a niece to a seminar on small business entrepreneurship. Several people were introduced who had started their businesses at young ages and had achieved success. One young man owned The Pink Dolphin Clothing Company, which my kids were familiar with. They learned how he had started a business in a garage with a screen printer and how his first order was awful because the dye bled everywhere. They listened as he explained how he tried again and got the procedures just right and sold his next batch for a profit. Screen printing was never on their radar before this event, neither was clothing design, but it was now. How many other possible careers are out there that students could have the opportunity to connect with if they just had the chance to see them and meet people involved?

BUILDING CONNECTIONS

ALL THESE TRIPS CREATE MORE INNOVATIVE STUDENTS WHO SEE connections where others may not. Many businesses want creative thinkers who can connect the dots. They care less about right answers. Give anyone a cell phone and they can have the right answer in 90 seconds. However, they can't look up a well-articulated question or deep thinking observation. When children ask good questions and are taken seriously by adults, who share their knowledge willingly, children become more confident. Field trips allow students to interact directly with those who have the information. They become empowered, and with this power they are better able to maneuver through the world and achieve their goals, whatever both may look like.

As homeschoolers, sometimes, I think we forget how much freedom we have to get out and learn from others, from places and from things found in our communities, and in the larger world as well. I know sometimes I think the education will come from the carefully researched curriculum and method that I'm following in any given year. While I'm not one to advocate throwing out the plans and the books, we don't need to be handcuffed to them either. We have so much more freedom than this. If we are preparing our children for the real world, then education should include the real world. It should move the learner outward physically and socially, as well as intellectually.

Field trips really are an effective teaching tool for those more concerned with how to grow good human beings than raise good test takers, who all share the same body of knowledge. Field trips help students to see the deep connections between the people and the environments around them. They help them see how people work together in a very complex way, helping and competing with one another. They emphasize how those things that may appear to go unnoticed are important parts of the world, how social issues often have more than one side and how basic human needs are the driving force of much of what people do and how they do them differently.

MEETING THE NEED TO BE CURIOUS

CHILDREN WANT TO MAKE SENSE OF THEIR WORLD. THEY WILL FEED off real experiences, asking for explanations, coming to conclusions. They enlarge their understanding and come to see the realities of others. We may think of the study, the trip and plan the basics but then should let the kids fill in the details. We actually don't have a choice on this. Children will notice different things, pick up different pieces and apply them differently and that is just how it should be.

BY THE WAY, IF YOU WANT TO MAKE SHIRTS FOR YOUR GROUP OR

family, we have found they are helpful when taking kids to a very crowded area. If you often go with the same children, they will become comfortable with each other and soon start looking at exhibits with friends or scatter throughout a hillside. The children are easier to find if you can just look for one color shirt, and that makes gathering them back up five minutes before the museum closes much quicker. Which reminds me, make your field trips long when you can. We went to a hands-on museum for six hours a couple of months ago. The museum was two hours away, so the students were in the car for four hours. Ours hadn't even finished all of the exhibits in six hours, which is fine since it's about connection, not quantity. It is better to go than not, but when you get there, spend as much time as you can. The "move-along" mentality should be limited. Allow for that slow mental progression. Just as we form relationships slowly, we need time to process our experiences. The real world doesn't always need to have an agenda and a closing time.

3

THE RESEARCH

"Since we can't know what knowledge will be the most needed in the future, it is senseless to try to teach it in advance. Instead, we should try to turn out people who love learning so much and learn so well, that they will be able to learn whatever needs to be learned." John Holt

$\mathcal{N}$ot surprisingly there are a large number of studies that have been done about field trips, some by educators and others by venues wanting to attract more students. I offer up a few of the studies so you can see it's not just me saying that getting out on learning adventures really does lead to some strong tangible results.

WHAT FIELD TRIPS DON'T DO WELL

LET'S START HERE, AND GET THE NEGATIVES OUT OF THE WAY FIRST.

That's almost always the best approach. There are some things that adding field trips to your learning plan won't do.

PREPARING FOR TESTS

FIELD TRIPS WON'T HELP INCREASE YOUR STUDENT'S MULTIPLE choice test score. Students on field trips simply do not all pick up the same knowledge even when the plaque is right in front of them. One study tested students after field trips and after lectures. It came to the conclusion that field trips do not help students remember isolated facts, such as the birth and death dates of Egyptian rulers, when upper and lower Egypt joined and the current largest exports from that country. However, it found that students perform better on more open-ended essay type questions on tests. They could describe with more passion, more relationship and more depth things like how the death of an Egyptian Pharaoh affected his people. The kids perform worse on these multiple choice tests, because these venues and activities can rarely deliver the same experience to each visitor. Most kids will need to take these types of tests at some point, so some other prep might be necessary. Unfortunately, multiple choice test scores are pushed so hard that it has been found to be a primary reason that public school students are going on fewer field trips than ever before in America.

Teachers and adults used to understand the great value in getting out and about. In the early 1900's, many teacher training colleges recognized the need to learn how to go on excursions and to do them well. Some colleges had an Environment Class that teachers needed to take as part of their program. They learned how to use what was available to them in their town to develop interest, application, motivation and connection to the students.

The teachers in training learned that they needed to help children learn by doing, feeling, smelling and seeing. That was many years ago, and I can tell you, in getting my teaching degree, using the real world to learn was barely mentioned.

GETTING LESS FROM TRIPS BECAUSE PEOPLE ARE GOING LESS

THE CINCINNATI ARTS ORGANIZATION WAS CONCERNED WHEN THEY saw fewer and fewer organizations coming to various museums for field trips. They sent out surveys to see if they could pinpoint the problem. The need to spend more time teaching to the tests was one of the major reasons not to go. Lack of educational funds was also cited as a big reason, but another big reason was the shift in thinking about why students should go on field trips. In a related study in Arkansas, teachers who had taught for more than 15 years still thought field trips were meant to extend classroom learning, to add an enriching experience to the topics of study. The newer teachers thought that the primary purpose of a field trip was to add a reward experience, to create a diversion from the heavy school load. Outings have become relegated to the same sphere as a break from learning when the research clearly shows they are not, or at least don't need to be.

UNREALISTIC EXPECTATIONS

BEFORE WE MOVE ON TO THE BENEFITS, I WANT TO MAKE YOU AWARE of what some studies found as another drawback. Field trips sometimes tried to focus on too much and were used to teach very complex ideas in one trip. This was often followed with very poor results, as far as the success of learning the complex idea was concerned. For instance, a trip to the Capitol will not result in a child understanding how our government works. A trip to the grocery store, with a discussion of where the food came from, does not mean a student understands the distance things are shipped, and the cost of shipping. He doesn't have enough information to be part of a good discussion on local versus shipped food and energy and economic costs. If we add some context before the trip and some follow-up after, along with trying to understand smaller parts of a large topic, then the results of field trips are much better.

WHAT FIELD TRIPS DO WELL

SO FIELD TRIPS WON'T GIVE OUR CHILDREN THE RIGHT ANSWER ON A test, or an understanding of a very large concept all at once. What does the research show us that a field trip does give us?

WORKS WITH THE WAY OUR NATURAL BRAIN PROCESSES

AN EXCURSION IS PROCESSED BY OUR BRAINS DIFFERENTLY THAN textbook learning or lectures. Our brain is always trying to decide what is relevant and what it can discard. Worksheets and textbooks demand students pay attention to things that our brains tell us are irrelevant. We can learn techniques to help our brains retain the written word but it is often more effort than other experiences. A child is wired from birth to watch, hear and interact with the environment and the people in it, constantly trying to find out what information is important. A real world event which is linked to previous information is seen as important and our brains concentrate better on it. For instance we may notice silver rectangular boxes on walls and even remember their locations after only walking through a new area once, because we have learned they give us water and we are thirsty. We learn when experiences are novel or new as well, although sometimes it is hard to focus on a certain piece of the environment. The novelty will often produce emotions which help us to recall things later. We will then link new experiences to the old in the brain until we build up more general ideas about various topics. To get new experiences to stick better we can also link them to something else after the experience. This brings the experience to mind again and makes our pathways in the brain able to locate the information with more ease and have easier access to it.

EPISODIC MEMORY

WE ALSO STORE THIS INFORMATION IN WHAT IS CALLED "EPISODIC memory." We view our experiences as a memory of an event, an episode. Because an event incorporates all the senses, it creates many points of connection within the brain, and we can recall it using various methods. Something we see, hear, touch or smell may bring it to mind. Remembering things connected with an event is easier than remembering isolated facts. But because it is an event, everyone is going to see it differently, picking up what they think is most relevant to them on that day. This is why we can't completely control what is learned when we head out on a learning adventure. All we can do is offer, and let the children pick up what is most important for them. I think many homeschoolers are often more comfortable with learning being less controlled and a little sloppy. When we are willing to let our kids connect in ways that are meaningful to them, we can gain all of the advantages of this individualized, respectful approach. And it is sloppy, full of winding paths, gates, and sometimes walls we need to scale. Many schools try to pretend it is a paved road, and you just roll along picking up each piece in orderly rapid succession. It's not. And just because we are less comfortable with it, doesn't mean it's going to do anything but wind and zig zag. It can't do anything else; we are, after all, dealing with individual people.

RETENTION FOR TESTS

STUDENTS WHO READ ABOUT, TALK ABOUT, AND GO ON FIELD TRIPS about a topic perform better than students who spend all their time reading and talking. In one study students who were taking ecology were divided into three groups. The first group studied their topic by going to a farm, pond, and nearby stream. The second group learned ecology by spending more time in the classroom with no outside excursions. The third group was the control group and were not taught in either way, but did possess some basic knowledge of ecology comparable to what the other two groups possessed at the beginning. The students who had studied at the pond, farm and stream tested higher than both of the other two groups. This was believed to be because the topics were obviously and immediately relevant. In other words they were able to connect the lectures and readings to real world events and the combination was much more effective than additional lectures and readings would be.

There was a similar study done where a group of fifth graders took a half-day field trip to a nature center, while the second group of fifth graders learned the same material in the classroom. The students on the field trip learned significantly more than those who stayed in the classroom, and they were able to recall the material 30 days later with significantly more accuracy. Another study did a three test sequence, one prior to, one three days later, and one three months later. The students again showed large improvements in the subject and retention.

FIELD TRIPS INCREASE CLARIFICATION

IN SOME CASES WHAT WE READ ABOUT IN TEXTBOOKS IS DIFFICULT TO understand in the real world. One study found students were able to explain their thinking and how they got to their results on physics projects much better after attending a physics workshop at an amusement park compared to reading about the topics in a textbook.

FINDING THE RIGHT TIME TO GO ON A FIELD TRIP

ON A FIELD TRIP, HOW MUCH A STUDENT ALREADY KNOWS ALSO matters. If a student knows nothing about a topic, it's hard for him to pick out where he should focus. A study in Israel was done with 296 students on a geologic field trip to see what factors might influence the ability of students to learn. The students, student teachers, and outside observers were given questionnaires before, during and after the field trip. The effectiveness of the field trip was greatly affected by the "novelty space," or how new the ideas, area, and the relationship with the topic were. When everything was very new and unfamiliar, test results declined. Students who had some familiarity with any of these areas before the field trip were able to learn quite a bit more. Students who had prepared ahead of time with an understanding of the topic, what they would be doing on the trip, and what the expectations were, gained significantly higher achievement and attitude levels. The designers of this study suggest that if students are taught some general ideas about the venue and what it will have to offer, they will gain more from the field trip experience. However, if everything is too novel or new, then learning is reduced.

BONDING AND OTHER BENEFITS

THERE ARE OTHER BENEFITS TO FIELD TRIPS BESIDES GAINED knowledge. In another study, field trips were shown to create more unification within a team. This can be true in a family as well. By spending time with others in shared experiences we are feel more connected towards them. In a team study participants felt like it aided in not only bonding with their team but personal development and gaining a personal relationship with the subject.

Another study found that students cared much more about a site after visiting, which led to more civic responsibility towards historical sites and natural areas. In one research study, the author states, "Based on the descriptions that these participants gave, field trips can have a profound effect on the viewpoints and memories that students create and carry into their adult lives."

Researchers at the University of Arkansas conducted a study to find out what students gain from going to an art museum. They concluded that art and other "enriching field trips contribute to the development of students into civilized young men and women who possess more knowledge about art, have stronger critical-thinking skills, exhibit historical empathy, display higher levels of tolerance, and have a greater taste for consuming art and culture." In another study, similar results were found. Students were more properly behaved in a variety of settings, respected other cultures more, were more knowledgeable about art, had stronger abilities to think critically about a topic, exhibited empathy for those who have different perspectives, had a higher tolerance for others, and a greater taste for consuming art and culture.

List of Benefits

Instead of continuing with all of the other studies and research, I will compile a list of the gains that I found mentioned. The appendix will have links to the research and studies if you are like me and want to go further into it.

The benefits of field trips include increases in:

- understanding of new material
- understanding both abstract and concrete concepts
- retention of information for longer periods of time
- bonds within groups
- awareness and sensitivity to other cultures, time periods and forms of expression
- feeling of connection and caring for their communities
- understanding of students' effects on the environment and how their actions influence others in the community
- imagination
- confidence
- desire to communicate
- appreciation for the people they see working in various fields
- trust in others on the trip

- leadership skills
- ability to develop alternative solutions
- appreciation for life
- self-discipline
- self-knowledge
- positive feelings toward learning
- physical fitness
- choice, responsibility and self-direction among children

FIELD TRIPS CAN ALSO BENEFIT STUDENTS IN THE FOLLOWING WAYS:

- In the area of arts and music, it was found that students could better discern and discuss what makes something a quality work and why
- helps answer the question of "why do we need to study this?"
- introduces children to careers they may have never thought about
- lowers teacher burnout
- builds excitement and connection to a topic
- math events in the real world have been found to help students gain a more positive attitude towards math
- makes art relevant
- reinforces the importance of creativity and individuality
- helps students to see other forms of expression as valid
- gives a real example of complex concepts
- provides a detox period for new homeschoolers
- hones critical thinking skills

- allows students to develop their own conclusion and opinions
- creates a well-rounded children
- reduces fear and negative feelings of people who are different
- gives a broader understanding and definition of learning
- introduces role models, who have achieved
- helps students become more aware of what's around them
- introduces other ways of doing things
- opens new paths
- allows for individual connection
- spark ideas to share
- students value human relationships and connections more
- creates a new attitude of looking for what's going on in a situation
- children with ADHD are better able to concentrate after contact with nature
- play becomes more diverse
- introduces hobbies
- encourages positive risk-taking

4

OVERCOMING EXCUSES NOT TO GO

"The whole object of travel is not to set foot on foreign land:
it is at last to set foot on one's own country as a
foreign land." G. K. Chesterson

When it comes to reasons for not taking the kids on educational outings, I've heard them all. I've probably used them all. Luckily, I've got friends and children who can't come up with reasons to stay home. A healthy mix of the two seems to be the best plan.

MULTIPLE CHILDREN

ONE OF THE MOST COMMON REASONS FOR NOT GOING THAT I'VE come across is that a family has multiple children. Having multiple children can make things difficult, but we don't need to let it stop us. This last year I had seven at home, the oldest being a senior in high school, the youngest a baby.

Going to places that weren't very crowded were the easiest and was the best place to start. When we started going regularly, I took just my kids on a teaching walk. They ran ahead and after awhile I called to them. Some of them couldn't hear me. I then set up a picnic and the ones who couldn't hear soon saw what we were doing and came back. We then talked about the importance of staying where they could hear. We talked about staying with buddies. We experimented with how far they could run and still hear me.

We do pair up on outings that involve crowded areas. Each of the older children will partner with a younger one and then I periodically ask them where their partner is. I've found, though, that my younger two would just rather stay with me. My youngest is usually in a stroller if we are on a walking around type trip, and my next oldest holds on to the side or occasionally rides on the front. I know several moms that use carriers.

Many of our trips don't involve long walks or crowds. If you are new, look through the chapters on ideas and start there. Also, if you go to traditional museums or venues between one and three in the afternoon, the public school field trips are about done and the after school kids haven't come yet, so you will likely have smaller crowds.

Remember that not everyone has to learn the same thing. In a large family, a trip might be more about what's on the surface for young kids, but more complicated, relationship and issue-driven for the older children. I want to encourage you to try a trip even if your spouse can't join you. Go somewhere easy at first, maybe somewhere where the kids can run in the open.

It is also often easier to go with another family or several other families. The additional friends keep the kids together, and the additional parents help keep an eye on the kids and give me more cell phones to text to see if they can see my older children. I admit to being one of those moms who counts heads every few minutes. I was worse when I had more littles than bigs, but even with four over 11 and only three younger, I still count. I've taken photos of my kid, before busy trips, in case they get separated. Other basic safety tips should be taught. Summers are for life skills for us, so we tend to review our safety rules each summer, including safety in groups, crowds, and on outings.

MULTIPLE AGES

A CLOSELY RELATED CONCERN TO HAVING MULTIPLE CHILDREN IS THE concern of going on outings with multiple aged children. We have found a lot of places to go that appeal to all age groups. They won't all focus on the same things, but they can learn many things from the same trip. Many times we have worried that a trip might be too young or too old for certain kids, but from discussions after, we found they were all able to learn many, many things. There are times, however, that we have left the older children at home, especially when they are busy preparing for plays, speeches or time-consuming projects. Occasionally it has made sense to leave the younger ones. Some venues don't allow young children. For instance, we went to a planetarium and children under four were not allowed, since people leaving during the presentation would be disruptive. We also have a local theater that is very small and uses the aisles often in their plays, so young children who might need to leave are not allowed. In both cases I have gone and just played with my little ones outside as my older children went in with other adults.

For the most part, though, I'd suggest taking everyone. When a family goes on these adventures together, and then they take the time to remember and share, they build a common point of reference and a collective memory where they look to each other to fill in the gaps. I can remember my favorite dinner times as a child were when we'd all sit around and say "do you remember when...?" There was something powerful in it.

Cost

SOME FAMILIES ARE CONCERNED ABOUT THE COST OF ALL THESE trips. In a Vancouver study, across several school districts, venue cost was ranked as a much bigger problem than transportation cost. That's true for homeschoolers as well. We feel like we can drive our students around, carpool with other families, or use larger cars, but the cost per student for entrance into an event can be a deciding factor. I'll give ideas in a later section for free trips. There are also places to get discounts, such as Groupon. For the last few years all US 4th graders were given free tickets to the Federal Parks for their families for the year, which can open up a lot of trips. Several venues will have discounted days or weeks. San Diego offers free entrance for children to many exhibits in the month of October in the hope of extending the travel season. Some library systems have periodic partnerships and give free tickets or discounted tickets to local venues. Many venues offer a discount or are completely free for large groups. In California, and some other states, we have charter schools that will help pay for many educational activities, including field trips. I know one group that has done fund raising. Don't let cost be an excuse not to go, just an influence on where to go.

So Many Things to Do

TEACHING MATERIALS DON'T OFTEN CALL FOR A FIELD TRIP AND, FOR families who feel pressure to complete curriculum in a particular time frame, a field trip can be viewed as a delay, or interruption to "school." We also have more learning opportunities than we can possibly participate in, more books to read, teams to be on, educational apps, websites and videos to watch. These things can all be good, but we need to remember that we control them, not the other way around. It really is okay to miss a day of math and a chapter in that book to go out and have an experience that will be remembered for much, much longer. By going on the outings, we place value in the real world and the real people in it. We show our kids another way to extend and enjoy their learning for their whole life. We empower them as they ask questions and talk to adults and others.

In the Leadership Model of learning, they emphasize a six month "no". Every six months they encourage families to go through their schedules and say "no" to things that have crept in and are filling their time but that aren't the best for them right now. Be intentional with what you let in and intentionally leave some room for spontaneous and planned adventures.

My Child Has Special Needs

IT CAN BE DIFFICULT TAKING OUR SPECIAL NEEDS CHILDREN OUT. FOR some, it is easier, because the movement negates many learning difficulties related to sitting still and staring at numbers and letters. For these students, seeing how things are used in the real world can be most helpful.

The novelty of a stimulus rich setting for other kids brings uncertainty at first and anxiety. But one study found that if students were able to visit the area more than once and if they prepared with pictures and an explanation of what to expect, the novelty could be reduced and the other benefits of the experience could be achieved. Also, the more a student goes on excursions, the more he or she learns what is expected and can relate and respond appropriately. It is a process but one worth taking.

As we look through the possibilities of trips to go on, we can pick and choose those that will work best with our kids. We may need to make sure that if a walk is long, a wheelchair or stroller can be used or that there is a place to rest and wait for others. We may need to be aware of quiet spaces that we can retreat to if needed. We may need to go on trips that are less than an hour. You know your child and what he or she needs. Work within those parameters and still go. In the second half of this book, I'll give you a year's worth of ideas of places to take your child, but adjust and use the ideas as a starting place for your needs. All our children deserve a full and interesting life. Firsthand experiences are important to healthy brain development and later learning, including quality connections to community resources.

I Don't Know Where to Go

Beginning field trippers are often perplexed on where to go. We can start with where we live. If we live in a town, we've got stores, and every store is an opportunity to learn something new. There are people with skills and interests surrounding us everywhere. As we begin to explore our world, we start to look at everything and think, "would that make a good field trip? I wonder what that person knows?" The easy, most obvious field trips are not the only ones or the most important. In later chapters, I'll help you to find places to go and give you a variety of ideas. Getting out into the world extends our understanding and broadens our relationships, even if it isn't to the big museums. We need to think beyond the traditional field trip locations and start instead with what does surround us. Study your local culture. Look for the hidden spots in your area.

I DON'T KNOW HOW TO MAKE IT EDUCATIONAL

SOME OF US ARE LESS SURE WITH THE IDEA THAT ORGANIC LIFE IS IN and of itself educational. If we are doing something in our homeschool as educational we want to know how to make sure the kids are really learning from it. You may be unfamiliar with using the outdoors and the greater environment as an opportunity to develop real learning. You may not know what to do, and how to make trips meaningful. The kids will learn, but how do we make it more effective?

There is a simple formula that can help: **Pre-teach, Excursion, Follow-up.** It is a classic teaching formula because it is effective.

Pre-Teaching helps students have a general idea of what the topic is and reduces the novelty, which can distract and interfere with focus and the ability to settle down and notice. Pre-teaching raises questions and gives thoughts a direction. There are many ways to do this, but the best ones start with the kids asking questions. You can ask your child to think of a question they want answered before the trip. They can think of it as a mystery to be solved, collect the data they need, then present what they found. If they aren't into mysteries, you can approach it as something new to discover and then have them show what they learned to others.

Pre-teaching may include; watching a video on the job of a marine biologist, visiting the website of the venue, reading a book about the ocean, pointing to the pictures and explaining what any new words mean, showing the children a sample of an aquarium you would like them to help build, brainstorm together as many questions as you can about aquariums. We can also get them thinking about aquariums by asking what they remember from an earlier trip or a trip to the ocean. Tapping into their previous knowledge and experience helps to give the new experience context. We want to get the kids' thoughts on the topic before the trip.

For older students, one of the best ways to get them thinking is to bring up a question or a problem that needs to be thought about from more than one perspective. Should a healthy marine animal live in an aquarium rather than the ocean? How can we filter garbage in the ocean? Thought provoking questions can lead to other good questions, thinking, and discussion about the topic of the trip.

We don't need to do all of these pre-teaching things, of course. If we look to the research, we see that it is best to do just a few before the trip. We want to leave room for questions; things dangling and not yet answered. Learning happens in the "aha" moments.

Excursion: The next step is to go on the trip. Take your time through the exhibits, stop to talk, ask questions, find answers to questions. If you want to take pictures, draw or write about the things right in front of you, a little of that is good. We have done worksheets at exhibits with mixed results. It can help kids to focus, but it can also stifle their ability to relate in their own way to what they are seeing and experiencing.

Follow-up: After the field trip, we should do something to help our children put together what they have learned. This can look like a good conversation at dinner. Children can add drawings and writings to their notebooks. They can build models and incorporate what they've learned into their play. We can read more books and stop to talk about how things were like something we saw. They can write thank-you notes that specifically mention their favorite part and what they learned. This reinforces the learning one more time, something a general thank you won't do.

That's it **Pre-teach, Excursion, Follow-up.** It can be as simple as, "look here are photos of the types of frogs we have around here," followed by a trip to a pond. After the pond, we may draw or write about which frogs we saw. We can also go more in depth, learning about the frog life cycle through building a model, how frogs can be endangered by environmental changes by watching a video, read a book about pet frogs to learn what they need and then look through guidebooks to find which frogs are in your area. We can then go to the pond and identify and graph how many frogs we see. We can catch a couple and observe them, try to identify what phase of life they are in, drawing and writing about them right there. We can create a list of questions at the pond, looking carefully at their environment. We can then go home and make a display board with our graphs and drawings, research the questions we asked, write a paper about them and then give a speech about all we have learned.

How in depth and which methods you use for the follow-up is going to depend largely on your educational philosophy and interest. Sometimes our job is to give an outline and let the child fill in the details. You can offer a choice of how to reflect on a field trip. The reflection allows the mind to go over it again and begins to make those pathways more permanent. If we discuss and then look at the photos of those moments caught in time, retention is strengthened. What the kids are thinking about is what they will remember, so if learning new software uses more mental energy than the presentation, then it is the software and not the content which is most likely to be remembered.

As kids show what they know through arts and crafts and writing and speaking, we can pull in so much more. When we have children tell us what they saw and what they thought, we are asking them to use one set of skills. When we ask them to write, they use vastly different, more reflective, and organized skills. Using different forms of the arts requires the development and use of different types of expression. Sometimes our children may not want to or be able to use words to express their thoughts or feelings, but they have a feeling they want to get across. In this case, we may turn to paint, or music and dance. This doesn't have to be formal. It can be silly and in your living room. Maybe you ask them to act out what they felt like when they saw the Stegosaurus display and then you ask them to act out what they felt about the T-rex chasing the Parasaurolophus.

The arts offer many ways to show understanding; helping children to understand that a piece of knowledge belongs to them. It allows them to demonstrate it to the world in many ways, or at least to those in their living room. This is the pinnacle for those following the classical education model, and one of the legs of many other methods: show us and show us beautifully; persuade us; influence us.

If we are doing this field trip thing right-that is, expanding the child's viewpoint, connecting him to his community and opening the world- then he needs to express it in many ways. We can integrate things like art, song, dance, writing and reading. But the most important thing is a connection to the child himself. Does she care? If we can help a child to care, we've opened a part of the brain that allows the learning to pass through all the filters. We have so much input that our brains must filter to the most relevant. When we care, something becomes relevant.

When they do care, what they come up with can surprise us.

Don't just ask questions and wait for the right answer. Try open-ended phrases like, "Let's talk about..." and "What did you think of..."

If we have truly engaging conversations about some topic with which we have become deeply familiar, the comments become deeper. We went to a transfer station where a presenter was explaining the magnitude of all the garbage in the world. The thinking process going on for a few children was almost visual as they began coming up with possible solutions and trying to figure out ways around the barriers.

These discussions help children analyze, pull information together, compare it; in a word, think. Maybe if we got good at these discussions, we could safely put away all of our critical thinking workbooks.

IDEAS TO EXTEND LEARNING AND FOLLOW-UP

HERE ARE A FEW OTHER IDEAS TO GO AS DEEP OR AS LIGHT IN THE Follow-up phase as you want.

CREATE A NATURAL MUSEUM
    Create a poster to explain an idea
    Present a project to others
    Write a new label for exhibits you saw
    Summarize what you saw
    Make a photo documentary
    Make a Youtube video
    After looking at a memorial, make a family one
    Answer a question they came up with before the trip
    Write a metaphor or a poem about what they saw

Do a two-minute writing about something related to the trip

Write a 25 minute SAT type essay about a controversial topic the trip touched on

Pre-draw what they think they will see, then draw again when they are standing in front of it

Take surveys and calculate

Find a primary source and read it on the same topic

Play with related props

Build something with real tools

Create an art gallery

Draw a cartoon or comic

Outline a cause and effect essay

Write a children's book

Create a blog post

Write main ideas as Twitter captions

Compose and perform a song

Hold a debate

Write an editorial

Cook something related and explain the connection

Design and troubleshoot

Event a chain graphic organizer

Write a story

Write an essay

Write a history book chapter

Complete a reflective journal entry

Hold an interview

Make a lapbook

Create a mind map

Hold a brainstorm session

Build a model

Make a video or slideshow

Design a pamphlet

Have a dinner conversation

Skype to tell a relative about it

Write a research report

Put on a skit

Write follow-up questions

Do a survey

Write a tribute or eulogy

Create a brochure

Add to a timeline

Create a Venn diagram

Create a web page on the topic

Add to a map

Build models

Create a field guide

Create online polls

PRE-TEACH, EXCURSION, FOLLOW-UP. PRE-TEACH, EXCURSION, Follow-up.

CONFIDENCE TO GO

THE SECOND BIGGEST REASON CLASSROOM TEACHERS CITE FOR NOT going on field trips is lack of confidence. As homeschoolers, we don't usually have as much pressure or logistical difficulties, but I think sometimes we lack confidence too. It can be scary to walk into a vacuum store and ask if someone could give your children a lesson on a how a vacuum works and how they troubleshoot it for problems. What if they don't like homeschoolers? What if they say no? Well, what if they say no? We know that not much will actually happen if they say no. There are very few truly negative effects from trying and failing, but there is a lot to be gained from showing your children how to ask and that they can learn from everyone around them. One mom pointed out that these are often magic words when asking, "We are homeschoolers, and we were wondering if..." Most people want to help teach the next generation and most people are willing when given the chance.

5

TIPS ON HOW TO DO IT

*"Better to see something once than
to hear about it a thousand times."*
Asian proverb

I hope by now I've convinced you that field trips are valuable, and you should let go of any excuses and just go. I'd like to offer you a few tips on how to make them run more smoothly and be more enjoyable.

SETTING A SCHEDULE

THE BEST WAY TO INCLUDE FIELD TRIPS IS TO PICK A SCHEDULE AND start going regularly. We go almost weekly, but I sometimes feel every other week would be ideal for those with other classes and co-ops. It would give a nice balance between at home days and also keep the momentum up for field trips. But I have learned quite well there are a lot of families who love to get out and about every week. Some families also keep a routine up by going on a field trip once a month. This can give a family a lot of time to dive into a subject and study it before the trip with some follow up after.

By going often, you can have a regular routine that works on field trip days. We usually try to have our meet time at 1 pm, which still allows us to do our morning school work and read aloud time, keeping our daily routines as consistent as possible.

If you are going to an all-day event or somewhere early, you may want to start the prep work the day before. Preparing a few things will help everyone concentrate on the adventure rather than the stress of getting there.

Preparing to Go

To prepare for a field trip, make sure you either have enough gas or allow time for getting gas on the way out. It's a good idea to map out the distance the night before and then add at least ten minutes if it's within a half hour and not during high traffic times. Add more time to your start time if it is further away, you need gas, or you will be traveling through areas that will have a lot of cars on the road. Have ready the map and phone numbers of the venue and anyone you will be meeting up with in case you get lost or need to let someone know you are running late.

Gather the Necessities

Lay out appropriate clothes and shoes, which somehow

disappear five minutes before it's time to leave if you don't. Get the tickets, or money for admissions, lunches, snacks, and camera. I've learned that taking photos of the kids doing things is much more fun to look back at than staged photos in front of the venues. By collecting the photos, we remember all the trips we've gone on and parts of the exhibits we've seen. Also, if you will be going somewhere crowded, it's a good idea to take a photo of each child that morning in the clothes they are wearing, in case they get lost, so you can show others what they look like and exactly what they were wearing.

Be Aware of Parking Situations

Do you need to pay? Do they accept cash, only quarters, or will a debit card do? Since I have seven children, we have a large vehicle. Sometimes the rules and needs of big cars are different than for those with little cars that can zip in and out of spaces. We went to San Francisco once and found a parking lot that said it was $20 for the day, which is more than I like but I couldn't see an alternative. So I pulled into the lot, and the attendant pointed to a little sign that said larger vehicles and buses are $50 a day. I told him that's crazy, and we turned around. We drove around and around and finally found a side street with few cars on it and meters. We scrambled for quarters and filled the meter, but I knew I wouldn't have enough quarters and so would need to find a way to get more quarters and come out halfway through to feed the machine. It was worth it, though, because I ended up paying less than ten dollars to park all day. The moral of the story: keep quarters in your car.

HAVE YOUR ITINERARY READY, BUT ALSO BE FLEXIBLE

A TRIP CAN BE MORE SPOILED BY A STRESSED MILITARY MOM THAN it's worth. If your event does have very specific times that you need to be places, set an alarm on your phone and have others you're with do the same. That way the phone is hurrying you along and not just mom. In getting ready to go, I have found that a Time Timer makes getting ready smoother. It is a large timer that shows a red face when it is set, and as the time runs out, the red gets smaller and smaller. It's a visual way for children to see how much time they have. I use this with a list on the chalkboard of what they are expected to do before the timer runs out. I have to remind and prod less when using it.

Don't forget to be flexible. It is always nice to be in as little hurry as you can. It allows everyone to sink into the learning and the trip more than when everyone is worrying about what they need to do next. Remember that we can teach the same thing in many ways, and there is more than one tool in the box to teach anything. Field trips shouldn't be rushed through to get to the other lessons and classes. Field trips don't get in the way of developing the child; they are often the best tool to develop the child. Sometimes when we are flexible, we get to see side adventures and have side conversations that add immensely to the learning.

Having said that, it is important that after we get ready on time, we prepare the children on what to expect. Let them know the basic itinerary for the day. Will there be playtime after, or is the whole thing serious business today? What behavior is expected? Is quiet listening expected when watching in a play? Or are lots of questions encouraged, as in a tour? Are they free to use the bathroom any time, or should they go when they first get there and then wait if possible? Depending on the age and behaviors of the children, explain to them what they need to know to behave the most appropriately. I know one mom who also quizzes the kids as they drive on things such as, "If someone says "Hi," do you look him in the eye, smile and say "Hi" back or do you run away and giggle?" "If a tour guide asks you to not touch something, do you reach for it and ask "Why?" or do you put your hands at your sides and look with your eyes?"

SAFETY

IN AN EARLIER CHAPTER, I TALKED ABOUT HOW WE CAREFULLY review our safety rules before our field trips, which is even more important when we are taking our kids out regularly. Our home-school focus shifts to more life skills in the summer times and each summer we watch safety videos, listen to a couple of Janeen Brady's Safety Kids CDs, discuss all the rules and procedures, and discuss many of the reasons why. Before any crowded trips, we talk about what they should do if they get lost, who to ask for help, and where to meet. Teach your young children your phone number and if they can't remember, put it in their pockets or draw it with a sharpie on their arm.

DRIVING TIME

THESE DISCUSSIONS CAN HAPPEN WHILE YOU'RE DRIVING. YOU CAN also use driving time to continue your school day and be produc-tive. By using travel time with purpose, we can learn many things. I know there are whole books on car schooling, but a few things we've done in the car are to listen to audio books and songs that we are trying to learn. I am blessed with musical children, even though I'm far from musical myself, but I love to hear them sing. I try to select a few old folk songs and hymns to learn each year and then I make songbooks for all of us. We watch videos of the songs and then we sing them at home and in the car. I know one mom who plays videos in the car and has the children fill out accompanying worksheets as they travel. I have printed out material from venues we were visiting which one of the older children has read aloud to us while we are driving. You can keep materials in pockets in the car. That's also a good place to keep those books that have pictures with detailed explanations under them about all types of nonfiction topics. It encourages reading just by doing that little thing. If you also keep clipboards in the car with paper and pencils, the children can take notes, draw and create games on paper.

After a field trip, having discussions about the children's favorite part, what they saw, and what they thought, helps the children retain more information. In the previous chapter, I discussed more ways to pre-teach and to follow up and why. But if all else fails, a good discussion helps my kids to be able to express what they saw and learned, and extends their learning as they feed off of each other's comments.

BESIDES USING THE CAR AS LEARNING TIME, HOW ELSE CAN WE increase the educational value of the field trip?

MORE WAYS TO INCREASE THE EDUCATIONAL VALUE OF A TRIP

ONE STUDY SHOWED THAT ADVANCED ORGANIZERS HELPED STUDENTS of all levels to retain more information and be able to discuss it in conversation better, especially when the field trip would involve many vocabulary words the students might not already know. An advanced organizer is a method of relating the new information about to be learned to something the student already knows. This can be through charts or other pre-teaching activities. It gives a framework for what a student should be looking for in the lesson to follow.

This is the same idea as creating pegs on which students can hang their information. Cyclical learning works this way. Students learn a piece of information, and then after a period of time learn more and then more. Each of these bits of information connect and reinforce what was already learned. The earlier more basic information is sometimes called a "peg" and the later information is able to be added to these earlier pegs. If your child already knows a lot about the topic, a worksheet becomes busy work. If they know nothing, then pre-teaching with one is valuable, as it gives context to what the child is seeing.

Discovering a little about the topic you will experience on the trip is beneficial. It creates this "advance organizer" or "peg" that allows them to more easily assimilate new information they gather on the topic. Doing this also helps formulate questions that can be answered during your visit.

Another way field trips have been shown to be effective is to use the field trip as the pegs to hang later learning on. Students may go somewhere and then use that experience as a way to relate to concepts being studied after the trip. This works well in increasing reading comprehension. If a student is reading about a child who had to wake up early to churn butter and the student has experience with handling a butter churn in an antique store or fair, the student is going to be able to understand the flow of the story better. The more information and experiences a child has the more new learning sticks.

Concrete learning processes prior to a field trip enhance the understanding of the trip and can help the students notice more on the trip and engage with the material on a higher level. This is easiest for students using a unit study approach. If, after each unit, the student is able to go on a field trip, the effectiveness of the unit is enhanced by the episodic and novelty nature of the trip. This increases the likelihood that what the student learned in that unit will be retained in long-term memory. This information could then be used in a conversational manner and as talking points in essay assignments and other flexible thinking activities.

In some cases, it is also good to add sketches and notes right at the venue to a student's own field trip book. This works well at things like museums that are not hands-on, as it gives the kids something hands-on to do. Charlotte Mason was an advocate for students creating a museum book, where they drew "artifacts" and wrote about them regularly. In this way the children connect more deeply with an object and notice its details, imagining it's purpose and relating to it much more than if they glance at it through glass for ten seconds and move on.

By encouraging drawing, writing and bookmaking, we are extending the learning into other subjects and breaking down the barriers between them. Drawing and writing also allow students to extend their experience as they notice and recall more details. They might ask more questions, leading to organic learning that is more likely to be retained. This asking of questions while on the trip also teaches them that they can get answers.

GOING EARLY IN THE UNIT OF STUDY

THE BEST FIELD TRIPS SHOULD BE DONE TOWARDS THE BEGINNING OF the learning process, and that field trip should focus on hands-on activities which can't easily be replicated in the home.

It was found in one study that teachers were more likely to use materials to teach a little before the field trip rather than follow up with venue related materials after. I have found this to be true for me too. I am better at pre-teaching and getting the children excited for a trip beforehand than I am at following up with learning activities after, unless it is part of the regular curriculum that we are studying anyway. I know several families who journal and blog about their field trips, which is a great way of not only practicing writing and keeping a record of what you have done on field trips, it also helps the children recall and internalize what they have been working on.

It is up to the parent to make sure the field trip offers something to the children's education. However, many locations provide guides to help with this. Some even have lending libraries of related objects that can be checked out for follow-up activities or online activities and web cameras.

TYPES OF TRIPS

WHEN PLANNING YOUR TRIPS THINK ABOUT THE CHILDREN YOU ARE bringing, but with most children, the most effective field trips are as hands-on as possible. Learning is retained to a much greater degree when students touch and experience, ask their own questions or respond to open-ended questions. Lecture type trips can be difficult, especially for the younger children. I wouldn't shy away from them completely, just limit how often you go on that type of trip.

Remember, field trips can be simple and still be effective. We met half a dozen families once at a city park. The park was set up to show Californians how to conserve water during the drought. We walked around and talked about the rain chains, the types of ground coverage best for water collections, artificial grass and drought resistant plants. When it started raining weeks later one of the families stopped what they were doing that day and headed back to the park to see how the displays handled the rain.

After our trip to the water conservation park, we decided to walk and bike a mile up the road to go over a new overpass the city had just built. Getting children out in the world to walk an overpass may not seem important, but they were able to see the creek go under the freeway, and the bridge go over. We talked about rules for bikers and walkers. We stood at the top of the bridge for quite awhile guessing which lane of the road underneath would have more cars during a set time. When the kids waved, they found that many drivers below honked back. Then they wanted to see which lane of the road had drivers most likely to honk. This could be a great opportunity to begin a unit on probability, but it actually later led to a discussion on human behavior and predictability.

When we got to the other side, the students noticed how the creek was the same and how it was different. They found frogs in the creek and tried to skip rocks. One of the older girls got very worried that we would harm the frogs if we threw rocks. This started a discussion and one family followed up with a bit of research and continued the discussion on our next get-together, saying they had learned that throwing rocks could be beneficial to the animals, providing you don't hit them, because it introduces air into what was stagnant water.

This entire field trip was easy to prepare and included a park and a walk, but the kids were able to leave with a lot of talking points and new ideas.

A field trip like this is hard to pre-teach, except for the water conservation, but it can be added to field trip journals, gaining all the benefits of connection, retention, observation, and recall.

LEAVING AND AREA

MY FINAL TIP IS TO CHECK YOUR BELONGINGS BEFORE LEAVING, CLEAN up after yourselves and offer some appreciation. Acknowledge the work others do for us, and thank the tour guides or whoever shared with you. This also helps to leave the larger community with a good impression of homeschoolers.

6

ARE OUTINGS IMPORTANT IN MY EDUCATIONAL PHILOSOPHY?

"The more that you read, the more things you will know.
The more that you learn, the more places you'll go."
Dr. Seuss

 e have so many options when it comes to homeschooling our children. I love learning about them all, and meeting other homeschooling families and learning how they implement one or another of the philosophies of education, but most often a combination of several. We have so much freedom in education and each family interprets philosophies in their own way and combines them to make very individual backgrounds for their children's learning, which is just as it should be. As I've studied and learned from so many philosophies, I've found that almost all have a place for field trips and each can give us a different idea as to how to make them meaningful.

CHARLOTTE MASON/LIVING BOOKS

CHARLOTTE MASON SPEAKS OF EDUCATION AS THE SCIENCE OF relations. She says, "The art of standing aside to let a child develop the relations proper to him is the fine art of education." We are asked to stand aside and let a child develop relationships with things, places and ideas. We should not take a child on a museum trip and then talk and lecture about all the details of each piece. We may give a little information; we may answer questions, and we may ask questions, but mostly we let the student develop his or her own relationship with an object, piece of art or location. She describes children as "born persons." They are individual people from the beginning, and we must respect them and let them learn from ideas and the environment. Let books and the world do most of the teaching. Miss Mason advocates keeping a notebook where the student may draw and write a little about the objects he sees in museums.

She suggests getting outdoors for as many hours as possible and studying what is seen. Students are to play with the landscapes in their own way and then learn to describe what they see. In this way, they are to learn attention to detail. If a child wants to know the name of a tree, he's asked to describe it, and if the description is not sufficiently detailed, he's asked to go back and look again. In this way, he's rewarded with the name of an object after he can picture it in his head. Again a notebook is kept of the things seen in nature.

Miss Mason also advocates teaching geography by taking the students out and showing them a lake, an inlet, a bay or some smaller version that can be found in the local area. By playing and running up a mountain, the student can better visualize the many stories that she will read about mountains and characters who live on them or travel through them.

Weather should be only a small factor; the children go out in most weather. In that way they can learn many things about their surroundings. She suggests that children under six should spend up to six hours a day or more outside. Eat outside, be outside. Get to know the local flowers, crops, trees, and paths. When a child has a deep understanding of her world, she is able to connect more deeply with others by drawing on those first connections.

WALDORF EDUCATION

IN A WALDORF ENVIRONMENT, CHILDREN SPEND MUCH OF THEIR DAY outside with no regard to any weather. A young child who did school out of doors was asked after a cold, snowy day, "wasn't it hard to be out all day in the weather?" She replied with, "What weather?" At a very young age students learn that the weather is not a reason to avoid being out and about, especially in nature. High value is placed on trips to natural settings including forests, hikes, and farms. Children work with wool and beeswax from a young age. A great field trip for Waldorf students would be to visit a beekeeper and ask him how he produces the wax and if it hurts the bees? A sheep farm or a fair where the students can see how the sheep are cared for, and sheared would also be a great trip. The wool can than be brought home to be cleaned, carded, dyed and used for various felting projects.

In a Waldorf education, natural science camps, state and national parks and a variety of places where food is grown are prized trips for children through about fifth grade. Overnight trips where the kids can dive deeply into an area and experience are encouraged in the fifth grade. These overnight trips are also seen as a rite of passage that marks a period of growth and new deepening into the curriculum the student is studying. From sixth to eighth grade,r students go to history reenactments, trips that foster teamwork, and challenging trips such as rope courses. As a student heads into high school, he should see culture, leadership in action, service, and technology on his field trips, to broaden his views and help him to move into the physical world. These trips, whether they are overnight or one day, are designed to challenge students, strengthen character, build confidence, and develop community teamwork through participation in specific outdoor activities.

MONTESSORI

IN THE MONTESSORI METHOD, CHILDREN ARE INTRODUCED TO IDEAS through objects and experiencing the world in a hands-on way. Children are encouraged to get outside. In Maria Montessori's original school she had the children garden, make brick, build modern houses and make their food. Children could see how their work was like the work of adults and could provide for their basic needs, encouraging independence from an early age. She advocated real world learning over imagination. Connections to real life will lead to learning. By gardening and preparing their food children could see the process from seed to plate. By taking clay, mixing it, shaping it into bricks and then building small buildings they could see how a house was made.

Montessori education is very much about letting children experience the wonders of the world we live in. As the children gain independence and dive into individual studies, the children can go out to explore the world in relation to their topic of study, to gather more knowledge, collect new ideas and dive deeper into a topic. Because the Montessori Education focuses on creating independent people who are capable and feel empowered, the children themselves can learn to set up the field trips. They can be taught to look at pamphlets a parent has brought home and make decisions about the best places to go, call to make the arrangements and set up the details of the events. In this way, not only do the outings themselves create valuable learning opportunities, but students are taught communication and organizational skills through practical life experience.

Many Montessori students gain practical life experience in the middle school years by running a business. Because of this, field trips to small businesses,, banks, stores, retail outlets, factories and wholesale establishments would be appropriate.

CLASSICAL EDUCATION

CLASSICAL EDUCATION IS KNOWN FOR BEING RIGOROUS IN PURSUING excellence by studying the trivium (grammar, logic and rhetoric) and for introducing students to the great works, or classics. Like most things in the classical curriculum, field trips may be very carefully selected for quality. Museums are a staple, as are libraries, historic sites, and high-quality musical events.

The child younger than eight is still building his basic knowledge of the world and can be taken to community events, such as parks, fire stations, zoos, and beaches. The young child enjoys games and stories, songs and projects. Therefore, trips with these in mind can be the focus. An older child is ready to soak in facts and details. She wants to figure out things, talk about them, and explain what she understands about what she's seeing. This is a great time to continue with zoo trips, but stop and read the plaques and ask for a tour. Museums are great for this age as well, along with many behind-the-scenes type trips to restaurants and factories. We even did a behind the scenes tour of the emergency call center.

Since children are seen as very capable and eager to memorize, this is the time to learn languages. Language focused trips could include going to an area of town where the culture is being represented or talking to doctors and botanists about why they use Latin and how it simplifies their job.

The logic age child is ready for contradictions and the harder aspects of the world. By opening the child's eyes to more of humanity, we can help the child through the adjustment that happens as the child is beginning to categorize everything and relate it to what she knows. This is the stage when a child will start arguing back, wanting explanations and looking for any inconsistencies in them. Political meetings, court cases, debates, and contests can make good field trips at this point, as do visits to help homeless individuals, animal shelters, and nursing homes. As the child is forming strong opinions, it is good to help him to form them with compassion.

In the rhetoric stage, students can become less sure of earlier opinions and more conscious of how to articulate the thoughts they have. Performances such as ballets, speeches, concerts, and theater are particularly appropriate. At this stage, the student is also diving deep into his particular interests and should be helped to do so by finding events and trips where he will meet leaders and thinkers in those areas, and see ideas lived out. At this last stage, it is appropriate to have the student articulate particular aspects of the events by writing papers and answering critical questions about the trips taken.

TRADITIONAL

THE TRADITIONAL APPROACH IS ONE WHERE TEXTBOOKS, PACING guides, daily assignments and tests are used. Should they skip field trips since they need to have lesson 65 done by Friday in preparation for Monday's test? What if they use an online program where the number of lessons is mapped out, and the student needs to get through so much material before the due dates? Remember, even traditional public schools go on field trips. Today, they are often seen as rewards after a milestone is over. By marking a field trip day on the calendar, it gives everyone something to look forward to and builds excitement. It can also give parents a bribery point for completing work or a reward for a project well done or a grade justly deserved.

Parents with children in traditional schools or using traditional curriculum can also use after school hours, weekends and holiday times to enhance their studies, delve deeper into topics and introduce students to more of the real world.

Remember, even in traditional schools, some lessons are skipped, and books are rarely completed. It is okay to miss a lesson here and there to take advantage of the depth and longer term learning that field trips have to offer. For traditional schoolers, it is important to remember: you are the teacher; the book is a tool. I've seen the anxiety moms go through when they look at a book in May and realize it still has thirty lessons. At the end of every year, I have to reassure many families that it is okay that they did not finish every chapter and every assignment in the books they are using. It really is okay to skip a lesson and head to a museum, or to see a Shakespeare play or learn how a radio station works. If you need someone's permission, I'll give it to you.

If you do want to complete all your textbooks or if your student must because they are enrolled in an accredited program that requires it, then you can look ahead through the texts to see how many lessons need to be completed. Often a textbook will have 150 lessons or fewer, and there are 180 days in the standard school year. The other days are often used to study for tests or complete essays and projects, but can be used for field trips as well. A half-day can be taken off for a trip here and there as well. You can also plan for field trips that will only take half a day, so that your children can still study in the morning.

DELAYED ACADEMICS

DELAYED ACADEMICS MADE FAMOUS BY RAYMOND AND DOROTHY Moore is the approach that states we shouldn't push young children into formal study too early; this does more harm than good. One of the goals of this form of education is to keep a student's natural curiosity alive. We can use the child's natural curiosity to help them grow in a more organic way while they are young. Because play and following the needs of the child through rich experiences that develop the imagination, curiosity and confidence of the child are emphasized, field trips are often a staple of this form of education. We can go to fire stations, petting zoos, hikes in the woods, kayaking trips down the rivers, and to see and touch all of the statues and outdoor art around town. We can take the time to stop and watch musicians playing on the street, or head to a large city to walk down the sidewalk and then compare that journey to the journey of walking down the sidewalk in a small town. We can take a bike ride in the country and stop and talk to the farmers and so many other things.

In delayed academics, parents have the time to introduce their children to the rich world and all of the beautiful people in it. Field trips can also be seen as giving a new backdrop for students to act out their imaginations. If children don't know how to play because they have become addicted to too much TV, take them out to a new environment; especially one with water. Beaches, rivers, streams and lakes are places where it is very difficult not to play and explore. This is good advice for parents who have children who are very much interested in playing too. The new environment, especially when water is present, is so inviting that games spring up with little to no prompting.

One family homeschooled their children by writing down the questions they had, posting them on the refrigerator, and then reading and taking field trips to answer the questions. Don't be afraid to ask experts and novices alike if you can see something they are doing and have them explain it to you; I've had more yeses than nos when doing this and many people are very excited about the opportunity.

UNSCHOOLING

UNSCHOOLING IS SIMILAR TO DELAYED ACADEMICS, EXCEPT PARENTS follow the students' lead all the way through high school. Children are taken on trips not only to spark interest in the world but as the curriculum itself. Children live a rich life, interacting, playing and working purposefully with the environment and their interests. Instead of focusing on school, families focus on living, with the goal to have the children be engaged and attentive to whatever it is they are pursuing. By taking kids on many trips and adventures through their childhood, they develop an understanding of ideas organically. There is a podcast host, on "48 Days to the Work You Love," who talks about her daughter's family doing something as big as moving to a South American country for awhile because they want to give their unschooled children the opportunity to see things from another perspective. When our homeschool group was on a three-day field trip to a State Park of Northern California, we met a mom and her triplets visiting the same museum one day. We got talking and learned that they were homeschoolers on their way from Washington through Oregon and California to live in Mexico for a year, to give the children the opportunity of learning from the world around them. You can't go on a bigger field trip than across the country!

Excursions and adventures are a big part of what can make an education in unschooling a success. While unschoolers highly value studying what the children want to learn, there is also a place for introducing new ideas to see if the child will want to follow up on them. Frequent trips with access to ways of learning more about the topics are perfect sparks for the unschooled child.

UNIT STUDY

WHEN FAMILIES USE THE UNIT STUDY APPROACH, THEY FOCUS IN ON one topic at a time and then study all or most of the subjects through that topic. Often a field trip will be seen as a valuable part of the unit. For instance, a family may study electricity by kicking off with an exhibit to a hands-on museum to try projects about currents and the uses of electrical currents. They may work at home on building electrical circuits using batteries, potatoes, and other methods. They may read about Benjamin Franklin and map out the longest electrical wires that have ever been laid and figure out amounts of electricity per hour different size towns use and compare that to what business districts use. They may look at Thomas Kinkade paintings and imagine what type of lighting is seen and then try photographing their house being lit by different bulbs and candlelight at night to learn about how important the quality of light is to art. Then they may wrap up their study with another field trip to a power company to learn about power in their area and what issues are being affected by electricity today.

Unity studies can be enhanced by field trips bringing the studies to the real world and local areas. Also, it is often easier to grasp a topic by going to visit something related to it rather than bringing it into the house.

EXCURSIONS INTO OUR COMMUNITIES AND THE REAL WORLD CAN have a valuable place in our studies, regardless of our philosophy or mixture of philosophies. Pick those trips that expand your child in the ways that work with what you are trying to do.

7

TRIPS DURING A PERIOD OF DETOX

"This then is the first duty of an educator: to stir up life but leave it free to develop." Maria Montessori

*E*ven though one of the benefits of field trips is to break down the barriers between traditional subjects, sometimes it is beneficial to think of field trips in those categories, especially if you have to do any justification or reporting. Many children who have burnt out in public schools need a detox period. I've seen students resistant to all learning, swearing they hate anything that remotely hints at it. Putting them directly into more schoolbooks can be detrimental to some children who for various reasons have been scarred by the traditional system. This can be tricky if you do need to explain learning in the core areas.

Field trips are a way to continue doing things to expand while giving new homeschoolers the break they need to detox from classroom-based, test-centered schooling. Like the European gap year of travel between high school and university, after such a stimulating break, students come back ready to focus again.

A learning adventure gives a needed break from the methods that were used in classroom situations, while still providing some instruction. In this case, focusing on one trip a week and rotating between the four core subjects will give something to report in each of the core areas on a monthly basis. If you also add in a little pre-teaching, such as videos and a pile of picture books on the topic, and a bit of the child's choice of follow-up, it can still feel like a good break while starting to give a well-rounded, relaxed bit of learning in each area. It is also nice to take students on adventures that will spark them in certain areas. Picking favorite subjects can reassure them that there is much to learn, and it is enjoyable. The same is true for subjects a child insists he hates. For instance, if you have a student that proclaims he hates history and complains whenever he needs to open a book about it, a few excellent field trips can change his attitude. Often after students have related first hand with a particular topic, they are less likely to resist new information, because they have some background knowledge, have had an enjoyable experience and believe they can be successful.

LANGUAGE ARTS

STUDENTS CAN BE IMMERSED IN LANGUAGE ARTS ON FIELD TRIPS BY using many different avenues. Maybe you can start with a bit of poetry, as this is not often focused on in more traditional settings. Free verse has few rules, which can be appealing to children going through a detox. Look through the calendar of the nearest bookstore and see when their next poetry reading is held. Also, look for poetry readings in meetup groups online. Most poetry readings welcome guests, as they are often authors trying to sell their collections. If there is a list of who will be presenting, you may want to look up the authors to make sure the poetry is appropriate for children. Sometimes libraries will do poetry readings targeted specifically to children.

Another way to study poetry out and about is to ask a poet to take you to an inspiring spot, describe her process and then have the kids write poems. Sometimes it seems daunting to contact an author or others we see who have specialized knowledge and ask them to share with our children, but I have found many, many times people are very willing to do so.

While you are out and about with the poet, see if the poet is willing to show them what types of things spark their creativity and how they notice details and feelings in nature and in the city as well as at their desk. Moving around will provide the novelty that will create the interest and retention needed. Another thing you could do is meet three poets in one day, one in a natural setting, one in a city and one in an indoor space to see the different processes they use.

Now let's say you want to introduce how to give a speech. The obvious trip, in this case, is to see speakers speak. You can listen to them talk about any subject, but by watching their body language, tone, and confidence, it becomes a learning opportunity for public speaking. You can also go to comedy events, Toastmasters, Town Hall meetings, TEDx events, and debates. When observing people give a speech, it is often about asking the right questions before or after that help students recognize what was going on and what tools a speaker was effectively using to engage an audience.

I took my children to see a storyteller once. She told stories that they had heard dozens of times, such as "Little Red Riding Hood," and "The Three Bears," but my kids even years later remember the way she told the stories. They talk about the expressiveness she used and how it captivated the audience.

We love listening to audio books by Jim Weiss, so when a local homeschool group announced he was coming to town and invited us to attend, we were eager to go. The first half was a workshop where he talked about how and why we tell stories. After dinner, we came back to hear him tell stories. Not only did we learn so much, but we also got to see that this master storyteller was a real person. It is always inspiring to see real people doing awesome things and making a living doing it.

To get kids excited about books, we can take them on field trips to libraries with tours, or bookstores to hear about the owner's addiction to books and feed off her enthusiasm. To extend a book, sometimes a visit to the setting of the book can be a fabulous excursion. You can also approximate a setting. For instance, after reading aloud "Swallows and Amazons," how fun would it be to find a part of a nearby river with a little island and let the kids play. By visualizing the actual space, the children are better able to relate, to think of how hard things really could be, and how they might solve similar problems. This goes for stories set in cities as well. If the students have never been to a city they might have a harder time relating. Next time you go to a museum in a large city, stay after to walk down a bustling street with your children, or drive through a couple of sections of the city to show them how the dynamics can often change within a few blocks. When we open our eyes to the possibilities we begin to realize a time of low-pressure trips can give subtle background to future reading and writing.

MATH

AT FIRST, MATH CAN SEEM A TRICKY SUBJECT FOR FIELD TRIPS. SOME people may have one of the math museums within driving distance; lucky them. They could probably go monthly for a year, concentrating on different exhibits and learning all about specific concepts. For those of us who don't have a museum devoted to math, many of the science museums have exhibits that readily lend themselves to math concepts. To get the most out of it, ask for a math concepts tour from the staff before you let the kids loose. You will be surprised how many times a large museum will have someone on staff who is enthusiastic about specific concepts and would love to focus a whole tour on that. The other thing you can do is look at a few exhibits online and find and discuss the math concepts and then go and view the exhibit in person. It will mean more if they have some idea what they are looking for mathematically.

You can talk about shapes at art museums; the Fibonacci sequence has been a favorite of ours. We look for it when we see pinecones or sunflowers and have even learned to see it in particular shells.

A lasting lesson is to go to a tall building and calculate its height based on its shadow. If you measure a pole and then measure its shadow you have a ratio for that time of day. If you then measure the shadow of a building or monument or other tall structure you can use ratios to see how tall the object is. How many students would understand the concept with a couple of hours of real life application? Perimeter and area can be taught in the same out-and-about way.

Children who ask why we need math might benefit from a trip to the bank. Ask the banker before hand to explain to the kids why we need money and how the interest rate affects savings or loans. You can also ask about how to open accounts, and complete balance sheets. We went on a tour of a grocery store, and the guide talked to us about the tight profit margins that a grocery store runs on and some of the numbers that that particular store has to work within.

You can add math in other ways, such as comparing animal features at a zoo and graphing them. How many animals have two legs and how many have four? Children can then create several types of graphs, convert to a ratio and to a percentage. They can also calculate ages at a cemetery

Our local amusement park does a math and technology day where they teach students how to calculate acceleration and speed. Remember that graphing and probability are math concepts as well and can be done easily anywhere there is a crowd. Using observations at a mall, you can tally and then graph various characteristics, such as at 10 a.m. how many people are shopping by themselves compared to groups of two people or more and then repeat the observations at 4 p.m. After you have the numbers, you can start playing guessing games with your newfound statistics.

Here is a website that gives further ideas for outdoor activities on math- http://creativestarlearning.co.uk/c/maths-outdoors/ .

HISTORY AND SOCIAL STUDIES

HISTORY FIELD TRIPS ARE OFTEN THE EASIEST TO DO, SINCE everything happened somewhere and almost every place has had something happen. A good state website will lead you to many local state landmarks that are within a couple of hours drive. This approach by definition will allow students to connect deeply with their local history. The child who is bitter about education may open up when he sees so much of history is just the story of people. We can take a year to pursue the history of our area, pulling resources from landmarks and historical societies.

Where we are, there were a couple of Indian Tribes that predominantly lived in the area. As we visit areas, these same tribes come up over and over. While we may read about the diversity of tribes, it is our local tribes we connect to and who have impacted us. We can see not only how they lived, but how they still live today and how it has changed.

We have a state park about an hour from us called The Indian Grinding Rock. The first time we went, the little museum was closed, so we walked the trails and saw the housing structures, looked at the large flat grinding stones, the lodge, and the ball field. There we read the description of the Miwok Indians' favorite sport. It is a game they still get together for and play. The game is boys against girls, but the rules are different for each. Girls can grab the ball and try to get it down to one end of the field, while the boys try to get the ball to the opposite end of the field, but they can't touch it. They have to pick up a girl when she grabs it and run her to their end of the field. My kids visualized that game and laughed at how fun it must be to watch. They also made connections to the people behind the game. These were not just some people in books. We began to wonder about their daily life. They had sports, and if they had a major competition, did they have practices? Hmm, how often do you think they would practice? Oh yea, and the muddier the field the better-I wonder why that is?

I still remember one of the three field trips I went on in elementary school. It was to a field next door. Someone had thrown out their garbage in a field sixty years earlier. There were a lot of pieces of mugs, and dishes, rounded by time. My teacher showed us how to use gentle brushes like an archaeologist to find these pieces and then to look at them and think about what they could tell us.

Field trips don't always need to be far away. A great trip we have enjoyed is to the local fire department. The first time we went, we had a great explanation of how it operated, how it connected with the other stations, and how the dispatch decided which truck should go out at any one time. The second time we went, it was to use their trucks in an egg drop challenge. We got to see how happy they were to do other things with the community, and how willing they were to go up and down that tall ladder numerous times for our group to drop our homemade contraptions from the top of the ladder. We also got to see what happens when they get a call, as they did when we had finished dropping the eggs and were checking to see which had broken. But the egg drop leads us back to an interdisciplinary trip and on to science.

SCIENCE

SCIENCE IS ALSO AN AREA WHERE FIELD TRIP OPPORTUNITIES ABOUND. Many museums are dedicated to science. Many scientific principles can be seen out in nature and the real world.

The point of a science field trip should be to let the kids engage with the subjects. For this reason, we don't want to rush them through if we can help it. We went with our whole group to an extensive hands-on science museum. This is the one where we were there for six hours and most of my children never made it through the whole exhibit. While I did coax them on when they became fascinated in the weather room for over an hour, watching the frost form in different patterns, trying to catch the fog forming and watching the ice float over the water, I had to tell myself several times to let them connect and explore. It's more important that they build a relationship with six exhibits rather than quickly walk past the whole two hundred that were there and not remember anything specific about any of them.

At one point we took a tour of a local university, and some of the families stayed afterward to see the botanical lab. We hesitantly asked if we could look inside the large greenhouses which housed many plants from all over the world. We then began warning the children not to touch, just look, when we were interrupted by the professor who said, "Oh, no, go ahead and touch, just be gentle." Here was a man who was teaching students and not just growing plants. A few college students were scattered throughout the greenhouses working on various plants. They were soon bombarded with questions about what they were doing and were happy to answer. At one point I watched as one of the five-year-olds beckoned one of the botany students over to see an unusual plant. The student's eyes lit up as she showed the little girl a couple more of her favorite plants in that area. Sometimes we think children aren't ready for certain trips, and so we don't take them. When I watched that little girl's eyes light up at being taken seriously when she wanted to show someone a particular plant and got a positive response, I knew that we were on the right track with all these field trips which included all our students from babies to seniors. They all connected to different aspects of the trips, but they also were able to feed off each other's enthusiasm and questions. In the mixed-age groups, I think it's sometimes easier for students to be enthusiastic and ask genuine questions.

One other field trip that made a significant impact on us was the two million dollar Bay Area Model of the California water systems. It was built to test what would happen if they dammed the water in San Francisco Bay before the fresh water was able to mix with the salt water. The idea was to preserve all that fresh water for use and not let it run out into the ocean, something our children thought was a great plan. We soon learned the value of models, and of running tests. Ninety-nine percent of the tests caused major disasters in the model, and so they knew they could never build it successfully in real life. Can you imagine if no tests were run and they had just built it? We also got to walk through the huge model to see where the rivers we visited from other trips met up with unfamiliar rivers. We could see how they got water from one area to the other and why we need to leave some of the wetland areas untouched to act as the "kidneys" for the whole system.

On the way to that museum, I had seen some people building a very large boat under a very large tent-like structure. I pulled my car over and ran in and told them we had about forty kids going to the Bay Area Model up the road for a tour, then asked if after we could all come and get a tour of what they were doing. All they could say was no, right? The person I first asked went and got his boss, who said they'd love to have us. It turns out they were in the process of building a replica of a historical boat by hand with the help of volunteers and when it was finished the boat would be used as a floating field trip and science camp for kids. We had a great tour from a very enthusiastic guide. I drove home marveling at how many things there are to see and how much we can learn from the world around us if we just open our eyes.

IF YOU ARE USING THE FIELD TRIPS TO DETOX, LOOK THROUGH THE other chapters and lists that follow. Find one a month from each subject and feel confident that you are helping to heal your children by opening them up to the inseparable connection between living and learning.

8

TECHNOLOGY AND FIELD TRIPS

"Tell me, and I forget. Teach me, and I remember. Involve me, and I learn." Benjamin Franklin

There are many days I love my technology and others that I want to throw it all out the window and live that elusive simpler life everyone online keeps talking about. How much and in what ways we use technology will affect our kids in this ever growing digital world. There is chatter about top Universities changing their admissions process to include students' digital footprint, and while this is scary, there is some sense in it. If these top universities are looking to educate the next leaders, the influencers, they have to look at what and who influences today's society. If we look at who fares better in today's businesses, those who have passed AP exams or those who are Internet and social media savvy it makes sense that the latter become the dividing ground for who gets into the top schools as it is a better predictor of who will do well in the business world.

Angela Maiers, a leader in education, goes so far as to compare a child who can't navigate technology to one who was illiterate in the 1700's. She suggests that the person who isn't fluent in at least some aspects of technology is unable to be fully a part of the conversations going on in the world around them. They are unable to influence others in significant ways, and doors will be closed to them.

Technology is not only important but necessary and likely to become even more so. We need to help our children use it as a tool and navigate their way through it. Field trips give us a perfect entry point to this in several ways. We can help the children use technology in the planning and in the outing itself.

CAUTIONS

IN MY HOME, WE HAVE REPEATED DISCUSSIONS ABOUT HOW TO USE technology as a tool. Like most moms, I worry. I think we do need to be aware of the negatives so we can guide our children through them. Technology can be very addictive. It can interfere with relationships and growth in all aspects. Children need physical movement to learn properly, and too much technology can hinder that. Technology can decrease a child's ability to reflect, meditate and think. A college dean recently complained of medical students who didn't want to take the time to study symptoms and evaluate which were relevant and which were irrelevant to a condition. They just wanted a database that would identify the condition for them.

As adults, we are still trying to learn where our technology can enhance our life and not take away from it. We need to find a way to take power over it and help our children do the same. We need to be intentional. It's like driving a car. We know they can hurt other people and us, but we have decided that the usefulness and opportunities that open up to us because we have a car are worth the risks, so instead of banning driving, we very actively teach our kids how to use cars safely. We give them reading materials, tests, and then private teachers. Then we spend many very alert hours as parents, actively guiding, instructing, explaining and watching our child. After they seem to get it, we sign off that they can do it on their own, but we continue to check on them. We think nothing of calling them or texting them to make sure they are safe, after each trip.

We can think of teaching our kids technology the same way. We need to decide the rules, safe behaviors, and boundaries they need to stay in between the lines. We then need to show them, then sit by them, then check in on them regularly. We also need to use the internet with specific purposes in mind. Just as cruising is now illegal in most areas, so should mindless searching be banned. Is it okay to take a scenic country drive as a family? Sure, and online these can be fabulous as well, but not as the primary activity, not often and not usually alone.

Virtual Field Trips

So while we must be safe online, we must also be online. We need to be cautious and alert, but still need to get on the road. Tremendous opportunities and resources are available. They can enhance many aspects of what we do, but we need to be cautious we don't turn to technology to replace our hands on activities, including field trips. A study was done at a university about the effectiveness of virtual field trips. The virtual field trip lost many of the benefits of real world excursions such as, tapping into episodic memory, novelty, unity in a shared event, ability to notice and respond to individual stimuli not seen as the focus by the presenter. Almost all students felt virtual field trips were a useful teaching tool, but should not take the place of a real physical field trip.

That does not mean virtual tours don't have a place. Especially when we are heading to a large venue that has a virtual field trip on their site, or we are visiting a famous landmark, or place with an online virtual trip. They are effective at pre-teaching concepts before a real trip. By pre-teaching, we can focus the attention of the students when we are on an actual trip. We are also able to give them useful questions that they may be able to ponder a few days ahead before the real trip. Virtual trips often help anxious children as they will then know what to expect. They also make a good follow up activity, where the children can find answers to their questions that maybe there wasn't time to get on the actual trip. Also, we can discuss what each of them saw and relate the slices given in the virtual trip to the larger piece that they experienced. It is also an excellent activity in comparing and contrasting real life and the virtual world.

Virtual field trips or less formal virtual experiences can also teach students things that aren't possible in the real world. As much fun as taking our students on field trips to Paris, London, Sydney, Buenos Aires, and Guatemala might be-for most of us it's a little cost prohibitive. But we can use technology to get a real flavor for many places we couldn't possibly go in real life. My children and I were studying about India once, and the topic of their traffic came up. The kids and I were wondering if it was as bad as an article we had read said, so we looked up a traffic cam in India and got to watch what traffic in a major metropolitan city in India looked like in real time. Armchair travel is valuable as a method of learning about what is going on in areas of the world right now.

But beyond the distant, we can also use technology to learn about places we may not have time or money to visit in person. Maybe you have napping babies and wiggly toddlers, so a day at the ceramics museum sounds less than pleasant. Many museums have virtual displays that you can visit to help you learn on these tricky days.

Other museums have experiments built right into their websites. While our local California Universities still say they won't accept virtual labs instead of physical hands-on labs, those virtual labs can still enhance and extend the physical ones.

PLANNING EXCURSIONS

BUT ONE OF THE BEST USES OF THE INTERNET IS IN THE PLANNING OF a real field trip. Many destinations have pre-teaching materials online and ready for you to use. Sometimes the internet has the resources to enhance an experience. For instance, our homeschool group wanted to see and connect with Old Sacramento. One of the moms found a scavenger hunt online that told about different places in Old Town and asked the kids to run and find many of these areas. So, armed with a printout from an internet search and nothing else a great field trip was born.

I just planned a tour of the different sculptures around town for our homeschool group. We are breaking into groups and visiting several of the public pieces of art around town and then creating sculptures from recyclable materials. I started with my city's website, found their art section and copied and pasted routes of five to six statues with the background information on the statues and the addresses. I then did a search for discussion starter questions when looking at statues. I picked a meetup location and asked everyone to bring recyclable materials to build sculpture after-a great field trip was planned.

Groupon and Livingsocial apps can be helpful in finding ideas and deals on events. Also, any community calendars and forums will help alert you to seasonal events that you may not want to miss.

PINTEREST

I'M ALSO USING PINTEREST TO PRE-TEACH. WE HAVE A FAMILY Pinterest page. I look a couple of weeks ahead at the next field trips we will be going on and then create a board of information, pictures, sites, worksheets, videos and anything else I'd like to share with the kids. I have taught them with other aspects of our learning how to use their own Pinterest boards, but with the field trips, I make the boards. As a pre-teaching activity this week, we watched several videos about what makes a sculpture and what is art. I found a video for young children, as my 6-year-old had no experience with sculptures and then I found information for older children. We then looked at images of paper sculptures. While I read to them that morning, I asked them to use our scrap paper and in any way they wished to make a paper sculpture. After the field trip, we'll go back to our Pinterest board and looked at more sculptures, some large and some small and compare them to some we have seen.

Pinterest allows me to save calendars, links to ideas blogs and links to specific trips and pre-teaching materials all in one space. I also have links to generic field trip forms that I can pull out if there is no specific follow-up activity. I can share my boards with others so that they have all of the information that they want; to go as in depth on a topic as they would like. I have also saved more general field trip inspiration about the studies and the value of the field trips, so I can occasionally remember why we are leaving our comfortable home and venturing out into crowded highways with nothing more than a GPS telling me to turn down various streets. I also keep a board about my area with just lists of ideas of places where we can go.

Last week we did a tour and watched a presentation at the transfer station where the waste in our city is first taken before it is sorted and sent to various other facilities. Before we went, a mother posted videos on the topic, word searches, and coloring pages. We were able to have a great discussion about our waste and how we can better dispose of it.

FACEBOOK

OUR GROUP USES A PRIVATE FACEBOOK GROUP AS OUR PRIMARY means of discussing new field trips and posting events, details and getting counts on how many will be there. We also post photos of the trips onto the closed group. The older students are then able to take the photos and, with the help of one of the moms, make a yearbook. They are learning to use digital photo editing software and are able to compare and contrast different features of different layout and printing programs.

We have also used the several document features for various trips. We can share docs with all the families attending. They might have information, schedules, suggested discussion questions, etc. and we stick it all in a file.

APPS

AS OUR TECHNOLOGY BECOMES MORE MOBILE, APPS ARE BEING developed to help us get out and see the world. There is even a Field Trip app, called "Field Trip" where you can give it access to your location, and it will show you hundreds of points of interest near you. It can be used when you have a few minutes to spare and can pull over to look at historical landmarks right then, or you could make a field trip of just driving around an area, and every time the app sent you a notification of a landmark pulling over and looking. It might be tricky to plan ahead for that type of field trip, but you could do some follow up by taking photos of the landmarks, etc. and then putting all of the events you read about in chronological order. Since this app shows the landmarks with their information, it could make a great virtual field trip about areas you are visiting or your hometown. Other apps can be field trips as well, such as geocaching apps.They may also just give more information. Our zoo uses a scanning app, called a Q code to tell about the different animals.

Handling Digital Difficulties

We need to take into account digital hiccups and teach our children how to navigate through them because unfortunately they are probably not going to go away. In one study it was shown designers, promoters, writers, and administrators underestimate the interference levels of using technology and focus instead on how well systems perform only when everything is working correctly, but that in reality often things do not work correctly. It is like driving that car into a traffic jam every day but continuously estimating your travel time as if the roads were perfectly clear. Instead, we need to think about ways to eliminate the technical difficulties and then to use them as teaching opportunities when they do occur.

We can preview sites and equipment before using it with our children. We can have backup plans, such as books from the library. On my Pinterest boards I pin multiple possible places to teach a topic, so that if one item is down I can quickly pull up a different video or tool.

Using Technology On the Trip

IF YOUR GROUP IS GOING TO SEPARATE WITHIN A SPACE SUCH AS A museum, make sure everyone has each other's numbers so that parents can contact one another, especially if the students switch around from place to place. Also, if it is a very busy public space, it is sometimes useful for each parent to a take a picture of the students they are watching. This not only reminds them, but it also gives a visual of what the children were wearing that day in case someone gets lost.

If families are separating over a wider distance, such as scavenger hunts of local historical landmarks, geocaching, and hikes the "Find My Friend" app can be useful as the parents can then see who is where.

Another way to use technology during the trip is to photograph what your children think are the most important things. I like to always include kids in the photos. They mean more to me later. I am making a photo album for my son who is graduating. I have more photos of him doing something hands on at various events, and places then I do of him actually looking at the camera, and I think that describes his childhood beautifully-very active and very hands-on.

Extending the Learning During Travel

TECHNOLOGY CAN ALSO HELP TURN THE DRIVING TIME TO FIELD TRIPS into educational time. There are several good audio book sites, along with podcasts. When my car CD player died, I was so sad I could not play all of our educational CDs anymore, but another mom told me that with a $10 piece of equipment I could turn my tape player into speakers for my phone. I can now play any station I want and specific lists of songs, speeches and stories over the speakers in our Tahoe. As we have gone through history, we've been playing the music from the eras we have been studying. This has added extra depth to our history studies. We've been able to see how history has a strong effect on the popular music of a time period. We've also bonded over songs and time periods that we have liked more and ones that we haven't.

If a car ride is long, you can also download movies on iPads and other devices about the places or related topics of what you are going to see. When we went to see the Golden Gate Bridge, during the ride, my kids watched a video full of facts about how long it takes to paint, its color, its name, length, structure and many more things. It gave them a lot to think about when they saw the actual bridge itself.

I have one family that blogs their adventures. The kids write about what they've done from their perspective and then add photos. Not only are they building their social media footprint they are learning skills that are just as essential as writing a five paragraph essay used to be. We can also send emails and photos with thank-yous to the various venues we visit.

We need to be safe with technology, but we need to use it as the powerful tool that it is. If we can teach our children to do the same, then we have given them a leg up on their future.

9

HOW TO SET UP A FIELD TRIP

"All you've got to do is decide to go, and the hardest part is over." Tony Wheeler

ower in Asking

I REMEMBER WHEN I WAS A HIGH SCHOOL STUDENT. I HAD JUST LEFT public school, and I watched as a homeschool friend got an internship at a very nice horse training facility. I wanted an internship too, and there was a western horse training facility down my street. I was scared but decided I'd ask them if I could work there for a semester. I thought the owner could hear my heart beating in my chest as I knocked on his door. Not only that, it looked like they were in the middle of a party. But the woman who answered the door invited me in, in front of everyone, and pointed to the owner, Lew. I asked him if I could do an internship there. He looked at me and said, "You start next Monday at 10 a.m." As I walked home, I could have bounced up to the moon-I couldn't contain my excitement.

That's how setting up field trips is sometimes. We are often very nervous, or feel like we might be disturbing someone, but in reality, we are often quite welcome, but won't know it unless we ask. Once when we were headed to an excursion I saw a group of people building a large wooden boat under a tarp tent, so I pulled over and asked if I could talk to the person in charge. I then told him we had about thirty students on a field trip visiting a model of the Delta and waterways in the state, which was just up the road, but I was wondering if after we had that tour, could we come and be shown around and see what they were doing. He said, sure, come back and he'd tell us all about what they were doing, and take us up onto the deck of the historical replica of a ship they were building. The moral of the story is to don't be afraid to ask.

Also, don't be afraid to be the coordinator and invite a group and not just your family at times. You'll get to meet new people, grow relationships and in many cases, the coordinator gets to go in free. If you are the planner, you are to be thanked and appreciated. So thank you! You are providing opportunities that other families might never have on their own.

DECIDING ON A LOCATION

THE FIRST THING TO DO IS TO PICK WHERE YOU WANT TO GO. LOOK for places that would go with what you are studying throughout the year. In that case, it might be good to plan out the field trips at the same time you are planning out what curriculum you will be using for your family. Don't forget to plan trips throughout the semester and not just as rewards at the end, although a fun reward trip here and there is not a bad thing. Also, remember to think of trips for each of the subject areas. Don't just go to the historical sites, but also do a scavenger hunt for local art in your town. Go to a play of a novel you intend to read, attend a concert highlighting the music of a composer you are studying, visit science labs at the local university, and attend a tour of a semi-professional sports park and then stay to watch a game. You may switch the novel that you would read based on the play and specifically study a composer because you know a concert is coming up, and that's perfect. The children learn that what they are doing at home has very real world value.

COORDINATE TIMES

AFTER YOU HAVE DECIDED WHERE YOU WANT TO GO, TRY TO SELECT dates and times. For us, because we meet up with a large group we always do Thursdays at one if we get the option. We sometimes don't get to chose and we do bend, but by keeping it mostly consistent everyone who goes with us blocks out their Thursday schedules. I have also found that Thursdays are near enough to the end of the week to allow for substantial study earlier in the week, and not to interfere too much with events and crowded venues on Fridays. By making the trips at one, we can get a lot of school done in the morning and then not feel bad if the trip takes the rest of day or if we end up socializing after for three hours. Field trip day is a good day for a crockpot meal.

CONTACT THE VENUE

NEXT, CALL THE VENUE AND INTRODUCE YOURSELF, EXPLAINING WHAT you would like to do. You will be surprised at how many places have discounts for educational groups. The school group rates are often cheaper than the regular group rates, so it is important to let the venue know you are a school group. I have set up a trip twice to one three-story hands-on science museum where the group rate is $7 per person, but the educational group rate is free. A significant discount by all accounts.

Ask the venue about maximums and minimums, how long any tour might be, can students stay around after the tour, when it closes, and for any other special instructions.

TELL OTHERS

NOW LET OTHERS KNOW ABOUT THE FIELD TRIP IF YOU WANT TO invite more students or if you need them to fill in the numbers for discounts. This can be done in a couple ways. I know I have circles of people I have invited to things in the past depending on how many people are needed to fill the numbers. I start with those we regularly do things with, then move to a couple of local organizations we are a part of and then move to the more general regional lists on Facebook or in different groups. When people you have not met are coming, you need to make sure to take deposits to reserve spots and to get contact information. I'm assuming safety precautions have already been taken on any lists you are on, they are set to private and the personal information of where you are going to be, and when, does not get to the general public.

You'll want to include meetup times before the start of any tours. It is always a good idea to ask people to be a few minutes early, but be aware in some places it doesn't make sense to have a large group standing out front for a long time. In these situations, you could have people meet at a nearby park and then drive over together.

Let others know any age restrictions. If the venue doesn't specifically say that young children are not allowed, leave it up to the parents. Homeschool children tend to vary more in what they can handle and how long they can sit still than other children. In some cases, this means students can be very wiggly, in other cases, students who have been on lots of trips and learn what is expected get very good at it.

In addition to venue, time, address, price, how many people, and age restrictions let parents know if there are parking fees, where specifically the group will meet before going in, any specific rules or expectations for the venue, if there is park time after and how the venue is to be paid.

PAYMENTS

PAYING THE VENUES CAN BE TRICKY AND NEED TO BE THOUGHT through. If the families who you invited are only loosely connected the reality often is many will cancel at the last minute or simply not show up. In some places homeschoolers are getting a bad name for reserving spots for large numbers of people and venues are dedicating staff and time for a group only to have a few people show up. One way to remedy this is to have families pay ahead of time. People are much more likely to come if they have already paid. Also, there are cases where the cost is a flat fee and if the coordinator pays it, then divides up the cost based on the amount of people who said they were coming and then collects money at the door, she is almost always out money, or she will have to turn to all the others that came and tell them since some people did not show up, they all need to pay more. Neither case is fair. The other benefit to having people pay ahead of time is that in many places there are caps on the number of people. If people take slots and then don't show up, other families had to miss for no reason. Because of this in some cases, it may be better to ask parents to pay to reserve their spot even if the venue is actually free. Even a dollar or two helps families to make an active decision and more of a commitment than without it. The money can be donated to charity or returned to the families who do come or used to buy a treat for everyone after.

It's a good idea to make it clear that there are no refunds unless the whole event is canceled. A participant can find someone else to take their place, but the coordinator should not be out the money if someone cancels at the last minute. Neither does the coordinator need to manage a bunch of last minute refunds, and exchanges-they are busy homeschooling moms too!

If you are setting up a trip for families you don't see regularly PayPal is the easiest way to collect the money. Everyone can pay you quickly using your email address, but remind them to make a comment telling you their names so you can keep a master list of who paid.

PREPPING

AFTER YOU HAVE THE FIELD TRIP PLANNED, THE INFORMATION SENT, the money collected. It's time to focus on the learning and the day.

If you find useful resources for pre-learning activities or activity books from venue websites, pass these on to others who are attending. You might want to send it with a reminder email one week before. It is a good idea to send another email the day before. In this email, you might want to remind everyone of any rules, special circumstances, and specific meeting locations. Our group has a shared calendar, and we create events for the trips, then Facebook will send automatic reminders for the events.

The day of the trip make sure you get there early to talk to any guides or make payments and to help everyone gather. When everyone has gathered, explain to the whole group expected behavior appropriate to the venue. For instance, you might need to explain any information, such as, if there will be a tour and then free museum time or if there are special rules such as we need to be extra quiet when we walk through the offices on the way to the overlooking windows, because the people at the recycling center are working and making phone calls. We want to spread a good image of homeschoolers, and every visit either attracts or detracts from that. The communities are more likely to invite us and think favorably of these field trips and homeschoolers as a whole if we are respectful and attentive.

Start the field trip on time, even if some families are running late. If you get in the habit of starting late, people will come later and later. People running late can catch up, but those who need to get in and out shouldn't be punished.

You will also want to end the field trip part and let parents know if they can either stay and look around or you need to leave. We often look to the planner to tell us if they would like to take all of the kids to a park after. The kids almost always enjoy the additional social time and running around after being so good for so long. Enjoy yourself. Try not to stress, but model the happy, inquisitive mood you would like others to have. Clean up after yourselves and take pictures. I love to take pictures of my kids and their friends when they are actively engaged in an activity. It helps us to remember all the events we go on.

It's nice to send a thank you to the venue after. You may also want to get feedback. You can do this informally at the park or send a quick survey in an email. You may ask, what the different families and ages of kids thought. What did people particularly like? What would they have liked differently? Is this a trip that you'd like to repeat? Would families want to make similar trips? Listen, but listen to complaints lightly. Different activities hit families who are studying different things or are less interested in a particular venue or particular topic.

My best advice is to plan one and go and then try to get others to take turns either formally or informally. If eight families each plan one field trip for every other week, your turn only comes up once every four months! That's not much work for a lot of learning.

GOING ON YOUR OWN

NOT ALL TRIPS NEED TO INCLUDE MORE FAMILIES THAN JUST YOURS. There are some trips that won't work with large groups and that is another benefit to homeschooling, we can go places whole classes couldn't.

One thing we have done is to have a surprise adventure day. I've told the kids we were going somewhere, but I wouldn't tell them where. I ask them to just get in the car and settle down for an adventure. I do usually tell them about how long the car ride is or else there are too many questions. But they have loved to be surprised when we get there.

Also, sometimes it is good to go back to a site your group has been to as a family. Second visits to the same venues can take the novelty out of it and lower anxiety in many children, leaving them with the ability to focus on what there is to see and learn.

A family trip can be rolled into your regular outings, vacations and squeezed into small blocks of time you may have. For instance, you may have an hour between a doctor appointment and time to drop off kids for a class. You may find a local shop to explore that you don't usually visit, a creek to visit, the oldest building in your town to look at and draw, or a train station where you can share a picnic as you watch the comings and goings.

When you set up trips for just your family, you can often just stop by and ask without a lot of pre-planning and coordination. It allows for a sense of curiosity and exploration and is perfect for those who enjoy their spontaneity.

10

I HAVE TO REPORT OUR LEARNING

"A child educated only at school is
an uneducated child." George Santayana

know some people hate the idea of having to report their learning. I have to duck my head when people start throwing the stones on this one since I'm one of those people that gather these reports. Let me promise you; it's not as bad as you think. There are many more sympathetic people working in these departments and for any schools that have oversight than the opposite.

In some cases, you need to report ahead of time and in others, you report after. The charter school I work with is after. I visit "my families," and they show me their work, and we talk about each subject and what activities they've been doing and then, in my case, I write the actual report for them. I scroll through lists of standards to find which ones fit what they have been studying. At various times I've needed to record the depth of knowledge, how they were learning and what means of assessment. The format required in the reports has changed four times in the seven years I've been doing this, and it's different for different areas too. Because of all of the changes I can't give you specifics or examples, look to locals for that. Instead, I am going to try to help you to report the actual field trips in a way that shows their educational value.

Remembering What You've Been Studying

My families, which currently include ten parents and 25 students, and I, use different methods to try to remember all the things each of our kids have been learning. In the past I have given each student a five pocket folder at the beginning of the year. It was labeled with the core subjects; English, Math, History, Science, and Life Skills/Special Interest shares a pocket. For high schoolers, I usually give them one with more pockets and labels that match whatever classes they are taking that semester. As students complete pages, they can slip them into the pockets. Brochures from field trips, little notes, calendars, lists, pictures and everything else that will fit can be slipped in.

Our school has moved to digital portfolios this year. These can be used the same way. Pictures, video, shared documents and scans of various papers can be uploaded into a shared Google folder for each student. If they are labeled by subject and date, they can then easily be sorted. There are a couple of advantages to the digital collection. The first is the video aspect, which fits how some children learn so much better, than stopping and having them complete a rollsheet. If a student wants to tell Dad all about an aspect of a field trip, grab the video camera and you've got an oral report. The other beauty of the digital porfolio is that the kids can add to it themselves, and they can go back and look at earlier essays, and earlier videos or pictures to see how far their abilities and learning has come. This is so much better than a grade.

Twice a year I have to build an official portfolio for the students. Usually, these items have to show something in the child's own handwriting or own voice and the samples the families and I have been collecting all year give me a head start. Of course, my families don't all use these folders in this way, we are all independent thinking homeschoolers after all. For those who do put things in the folders, it really helps when we sit down to look at what they have been doing each month. You can do this for yourself too if you are the one that writes the report. As you pull things out, they will jog your memory of what you've been studying and different things you've learned.

My families use various other methods to remember what they've done, which is half the battle to creating the reports. Some take photos of everything, Lego creations, hands-on museums, nature walks-everything. We then scroll the photos to jog our memories. I say 'our' because my kids are often doing things with the other students I work with, but I forget just as much as anyone else. We also look through calendars. I have one mom who writes a summary each night and another that just keeps a running document and adds things to it throughout the month.

If you are more technology based you can dump notes in another Google drive and share them with relevant people or use EverNote as a collection place.

As you are sorting through your notes and samples in whatever format works best for you, it might be a good idea to have the standards for your area nearby. Now I admit to occasionally glazing over on my twenty-fifth report for the month. But I have also learned the standards can be pretty helpful in giving ideas and jogging my memory. We have a standard about bouncing a balloon in the air with a paddle-hey, I didn't write them. My kids might do that at a birthday party, and I would never think to report something like that, but it's in the standards and so is the wording to make it sound all teacher-speak. You can find standards here in the appendix.

EDUCATIONESE

SINCE WE ARE TALKING OF TEACHER-SPEAK OR EDUCATIONESE AS IT IS sometimes called; it can be useful to know some. If your child went on a trip that involved both science and history, then they participated in a cross-curricular learning activity with a focus on... If your child told you about something and you asked them questions, they engaged in oral narrations in response to verbal prompts. Did they attend a park day that included kids of various levels and abilities? They developed social skills with students of various physical and intellectual abilities in a real world inclusive setting. Watching your child to see if they understood becomes informal assessment based on observation.

AS YOU WRITE YOUR REPORTS, LOOK AT THE LIST BELOW TO SEE IF any of the things you did on your field trips apply.

- worked in collaborative groups
- participated in scientific observation
- created
- evaluated
- analyzed
- applied
- understood
- remembered

- learned through inquiry instruction (student seeks their own answers)
- was informally assessed
- collected
- self-evaluated
- direct-instruction(being explicitly taught, usually in a verbal way)
- described
- summarized
- read expository text in relation to... (labels on exhibits)
- found relevant information for...
- identified resources
- used hands-on manipulatives
- built critical thinking skills
- designed
- occupational education
- increased stamina and ability in solving a problem
- key details
- compared and contrasted
- described how people and events are connected
- increased vocabulary related to
- made connections with prior knowledge
- found meaning in graphs, models, tables
- identified sequence or cause/effect
- found connections between
- provided reasons that support opinions
- used research materials and previous knowledge to participate in a group discussion
- responded appropriately to speakers and displays
- identified real-life connections between words and how they are used
- identified evidence, inferences, and opinions

- evaluated differing points of view and the evidence and examples for each
- identified research questions
- conducted short research projects to answer questions
- identified primary and secondary sources
- came to reasonable conclusions based on evidence
- determined the meaning of symbols, key terms, etc.
- identified point of view
- identified source of information
- moved through open spaces and avoided obstacles
- manipulated an object
- performed a series of physical movements
- sustained continuous movement for increasing period of time
- set personal short term goals
- collected data and record progress
- respected individual differences
- applied and extended previous understanding
- reasoned abstractly and quantitatively
- persevered in solving problems
- attend to precision
- identified and used structure
- used appropriate tools
- discussed examples of
- identified geographical features and their effects on historical events
- described why a fort, mission, computer etc. was established
- used first person information to establish how something changed
- learned how ...
- identified absolute location on maps

- analyzed how advantages and disadvantage change over time
- analyzed the effects of a historical event on daily life
- described the growth of water, education, transportation system
- identified the effects of various cultures
- learned to design and build
- learned sequential steps
- developed a testable question
- classified
- identified parts of an investigation
- collected information
- described ways in which dancers, singers, artists, communicate ideas and moods
- identified music from diverse cultures
- discussed how several artistic disciplines combine to produce a complete work
- critique performance

HOPEFULLY, THIS LIST WILL HELP YOU WITH IDEAS NOT ONLY OF HOW to write your reports but how different trips can lead to learning and small tweaks that can pull in even more ideas.

PART II

Ideas of
Where to Go

11

WHERE TO FIND PLACES TO GO

"The observant child should be put in the way of things worth observing." Charlotte Mason

I can't possibly tell you everywhere you can go on a field trip in your local area, but I will try in this chapter to give you starting places to look. In the next chapters, I'll give you ideas for two field trips a month for a year for several specific situations.

SO WHERE CAN YOU LOOK TO FIND TRIPS?

SPECIAL **LIBRARY EXHIBITS** AND **PRESENTATIONS.** MOST LIBRARY systems have online **calendars** that you can access and search to find things like author presentations, magic shows, puppet shows, poetry readings, Lego building days and exhibits. Our libraries also rotate and share **art**, which makes a good field trip. Also, some libraries have so much more than access to free books. We have a local library that has a free 3D printer and free classes on how to use it. A tour of the library itself by a librarian also makes a good trip. Check your websites and talk to your librarians, not only at your local library but find out what resources are available at any libraries within an hours drive.

Government buildings offer a lot of possibilities. You can get tours of **city hall**, the **capital** of your state, **police stations, fire stations.** We've even toured an **emergency call center.** Our town has acquired many original works of **art.** They list these online, so we went on a scavenger hunt trying to find certain pieces. One fascinating piece was back in a private area of the city hall, but because we came in with an intent to find that one piece we were taken in very quietly and they showed it to us. We also stopped and looked at **aerial maps of our city**, and each found where we lived in relation to other areas we know.

Colleges and **University tours** with a guide or as a family offer great field trips themselves. By doing a search for a local college or university and then finding their events **calendar** you will be able to plug into the many opportunities available. Many offer **lectures** that they open up to the public. We've gone to business lectures, and I've seen art and medical lectures as well. There are also often **art departments** with changing exhibits. If you look at the end of the semester, you are likely to be able to see **music** and **drama performances.** By looking at the calendars of just two local schools I see we could go; to an exhibit in the arboretum about the chemistry found in plants, in the areas of wine, perfume, medicinal properties and tree defenses, a photography exhibition on justice, a design competition, an exhibition on Australian Aboriginal printmaking, a speaking series representing Asian Pacific Islanders, a plant breeding lecture, a wiffleball tournament, a lecture on the brain and decision making, a seminar on how to assess the welfare of elephants, a debate on plants and patents, a lecture on finding interest in micro-history topics, a workshop on preventing human trafficking, the science and philosophy of Star Wars, how to prepare for a job interview, question and answer session about choice and sustainability, a student movie screening, a discussion about the proper place of mobile devices, biodiversity on the Earth talk and discussion, presentation by a food literacy center, a writer's conference and a child development open house. Those are all the things this week.

Many universities also have **long-term exhibits** or **mini museums** that you can visit at any time as well. One of the local ones opens their greenhouses with their unique plant exhibits; they have an **entomology exhibit, bird sanctuary, cattle barns, horse training facilities, vet centers, a vast library, arboretum** and **several nature paths.** All of these could be a field trip, and they can also help your children be comfortable on college campuses.

Museums are the easy, classic, go-to field trip. They are set up to be a field trip, so large groups are usually well provided for and tour guides are prevalent. Museums often have interactive websites, printouts and lesson plans. Don't be afraid to go to some of the more **obscure museums.** In our town we have an auto museum with a display of an original model T inside a closed room where the tour guide explains how Henry Ford was so smart that he designed and built a car, but he forgot that it would be bigger than the door when he was finished, and so he had to break part of the wall to get it out. We have museums of medicine, art, science, Native Americans, aircraft and many, many more. While most children really enjoy the hands-on museums, be aware that the hands-on museums can get loud and crowded, so for maximum benefit call and ask the museum when they are the least busy. It's worth going when it will be quieter, and your children can have many of the exhibits to themselves.

Nature Preserves and **farms.** Nature preserves are small to medium sized plots of land that are intended to be kept as wildlife and not developed. Often they are set aside because they house some type of animal that is being watched, or they are on migratory routes. We have a **bird sanctuary** about fifteen minutes from our house and have been able to go at sunset to see the birds that are on the water during the day head to the trees and fields to sleep and birds that are in the fields during the day come into the water to sleep. Many nature preserves have small museums with information about the local wildlife. This is a perfect time to bring nature journals and to take a quiet hike and stop to sketch what you see.

People often think of **pumpkin farms** as field trips during October. And because these farms are open and available this is often an easy time to go. But don't be afraid to ask these farms if you can come off season too. We have a farm that does a **tour** during other times of the year, where they show the students how every part of a hamburger is grown and made and then everyone eats a hamburger. We have also gotten permission from a pumpkin farm to come in July and go **blackberry picking** along their property edge. Other farms are designed as you-pick experiences. Another large farm I know lets volunteers come in after harvest and **glean** the leftovers for the local **food bank** and also allows each person to take home a bag full of produce. Don't forget more unusual type farms too. We found a tour of a **sturgeon farm** quite interesting. You could also try **dairy farms, wheat, and small family farms.**

Parks, snow, federal and **state parks** also make great field trips. Many parents do meet up groups with their young children at parks. These can still be fun as your children grow older especially if you come across interesting and unusual parks. In the winter it is fun to head to snow parks and ski, snowboard, sled or just play. Also in the snow you can continue with nature journals and study the animals, tracks and plants found. Federal and state parks can be beautiful places for outdoor learning. We often think of them as places to **hike** and see the forest, at least I did until I started going more regularly. Many of these parks have **historic homes** and **rangers** and **guides** who are willing to tell you about the history of the area. Many federal parks also have a **Junior Ranger program**. If you visit the **rangers station**, they will give you a booklet with activities. As you tour the park, your children can fill out the booklet and then take it back to the ranger who will ask them questions about what they learned and have the children recite a pledge and then give them a Junior Ranger Badge. I know one mom who has made a sash for her children who are collecting the badges and sewing them on o their sash to remember all of the places they've been.

Water is a natural place to explore. Every child should visit **lakes, rivers, streams, creeks, ponds** and if possible the **ocean.** These make perfect summertime adventures. My husband likes to look at a map of the foothills and mountains within a couple of hours of where we live point to a **dam** with water, look at it on Google Earth and then say, "we're going there." And then we do. We have had some of our favorite adventures by driving out and following creeks to various small public dams. Obviously, before you go, make sure the area is a public area and make sure it is safe for your vehicle as some are quite a ways out on **old dirt roads.** Many rivers have **bike trails** along them, which is a perfect way to explore those areas. Little creeks are nice to find as children can often get more intimate with the plants and animals in slow moving currents of a creek. We've seen beavers and otters in creeks near our homes. It is so fun for the kids to get little glimpses of the animals.

Presentations come in many forms and can offer a wide variety of trips. I like to have my children participate in a **play** every few years which means we all get to go and watch siblings.

We also love professional plays and think one every four or five months a must.

A few years ago I took my older five children to a **concert** by the Sacramento Philharmonic. It was the life story and works of Gershwin. They not only played his music, but they also showed video clips and pictures of his life and had some members of the ballet company and opera company participate with singing and some dancing. I asked my seven-year-old at intermission what he thought of it, and he looked at me with a very serious expression and said, "I can't imagine anyone not loving this." We had a lot of renewed interest in piano for months as well. Other types of concerts and **musical performances** are worth attending. Fairs will often have folk music, and bluegrass, along with other popular types. It is a good idea to take children to a variety of live performances as well as have them listen to a variety of music, so they don't get stuck in one genre when they come to their teen years.

Ballets and **dances** also fall into this category. We got to see a professional version of Nutcracker once and then got to talk to one of the ballerina's. **Square dancing** and other forms of dancing make great field trips as well. Seeing the different dancing and music gives background to references, conversations and books that help students understand more about their history, and what people have done for entertainment before technology.

You may also have an opportunity to see other **homeschoolers present** something. If you do, take the chance when you can. We have local groups that present parts of **Shakespeare plays, talent shows, piano recitals** and recently went to an **Egyptian show and tell.**

An occasional **movie** can be thrown into this category as well. In the summer my kids go to the $1 movies, and we still have an old-fashioned **drive-in** theater in our area along with an Imax 3D theater. Remember to ask for educational discounts. Many theaters have them as well.

Another category is **businesses**. This includes **grocery store tours** where your younger children can learn that the mango is the most popular fruit outside the US, and your older children can learn about the difficulties of running a business on a very small profit margin. We have done a **tour** of parts of a **hospital, a vet's office, a TV production station**, and even a **mall**. Tours to these places can teach you more than you can often learn by just going to them yourself. If your child has a particular interest in a company, see if you can get a tour. When you are somewhere, don't forget to talk to everyone. The **custodian** has an important job too. At our trip to the **transfer station** where our garbage is sorted and sent on to different destinations. We learned how complicated this situation could be and how the companies are grappling with the massive problem of human waste. As you visit businesses, you will find your children taking fewer people for granted and seeing how everything is so interconnected in a city or town.

Non-profits and **service entities** want to get information about themselves out to the community. It is inspiring to talk to people who see a problem, have a desire to help with it, then implement the plan. It empowers your children too, to see that they can change things that need to be changed. They can advocate for others, and they are powerful. We have been able to talk to an older gentleman involved with getting supplies for refugees and then make kits for them. The impact on the hearts of our children can be huge. We have had the chance to help in **public gardens**, visited the elderly in **nursing homes**, participate in **community beautification opportunities**, and **pick up trash** at our parks. Children who have picked up garbage for others are much less likely to be careless and litter. They need to see that someone needs to do the work, but it would be easier if everyone would keep things tidy beforehand.

Fitness venues and **activities** make good trips too. We have **gone skating, ice skating,** to **trampoline warehouses, gymnastics centers,** and **archery ranges.** This year I led a **running club** and got ribbons for everyone who ran a 5k, 10k, and half marathon over the course of twelve weeks. We then got a group together and ran the last 1.2 miles and those who had completed and logged 25 miles previously got blue ribbons for the marathon. Other fitness field trips can be to go and **watch games,** whether they are high school, semi-professional or professional. It is much more fun to watch if your kids know the rules and the point of the game before you go.

In addition to going places, you can invite **people to come to you.** Do you know **returned missionaries** or **world travelers?** Invite them with their pictures and slideshows to bring the field trip to you. You can also create events that are not exactly field trips but could be for others. We have done **history wax museums** where everyone studied a historical person and then created posters, wrote reports and dressed up as the person. As people came around, they told about their character over and over. You can do **science fairs** and **talent shows.** Many **libraries** or **churches** have large rooms that you can use for free. We have done a **recycled art day** at the park, where parents brought in items and students made sculptures, windmills, and even a rocket ship. It went much better than I thought it would.

Other places to find field trips are on **community websites** and **calendars.** Your local **visitors center** might have things that you haven't thought of, as do **local historical societies** and **chambers of commerce.** Local **parenting magazines** and **newspapers** will often list **special events at local venues.** Start collecting a list of local places and you soon may find you have more ideas than weeks in the year.

12

WHERE CAN I TAKE MY LITTLES?

"Education is a natural process carried out by
the child and is not acquired by listening to
words but by experiences in the environment."
Maria Montessori

*I*n some cases taking little children out on field trips is the most rewarding. They haven't seen much yet, and everything is fascinating. We get to relive it all through their eyes as we anticipate their reactions and just as excitedly tell them to look here, and then watch them turn around and tell us to look, look, look! Here are a years worth of field trips, at two a month, for them.

1. **Library storytime** is a given. Nothing is more important than introducing the young homeschooled child to the wonders of the library and story time which are often followed by a craft. It is a great way for them to get to know their librarian and the range of books available. When my oldest were little, we often went to

storytime in another language as well to not only introduce it but to broaden their perspective.

2. The **zoo** is a classic and for good reason. Remember not to hurry your little ones, a long observation of a few animals may be much more important than short glimpses of them all. Although, if they are still happy certainly see them all. Remember more animals will be out on cool days so try to go when the weather is under 80 degrees.

3. A **farm** is a must for a young child as it introduces the process of how our food is grown and gives context to what they see at the grocery store. It may be hard to find the idyllic farm with the variety of animals and crops that are in the children's picture books; a **pumpkin patch** or **u-pick farm** will do.

4. Our town is named after a **creek**, but the smaller town I grew in had access to creeks as well. For young children, a creek is better than a river, and the movement of it is more enthralling than even a pond. Though both are likely to have frogs, dragon-flies and other wildlife which are sure to delight. This is a good trip to take each season to compare and contrast everything going on.

5. Little children are often oblivious to the amount of garbage we produce, so a trip to the **dump** can be a real eye opener.

6. After they see and smell the problem of our garbage help them see a piece of the solution at the **recycling center.**

7. I mentioned the **grocery store** earlier, but I'm not sure I would count your weekly grocery run as a true field trip, but if we go deeper it can be. Can you catch the trucks as they deliver goods to the grocery store? What about a non-employee stocking shelves? Many will also do actual **tours** where they take you through the back rooms and freezers.

8. A **local bakery** is a delightful place to learn about the different types of bread we eat. We have a variety of bakeries with

various cultural bents. Food is the perfect introduction to different cultures for young children.

9. **Orchards** further help children understand our food systems. We have an area north of us that specializes in apples and gives tours and tasty treats. We've also driven up for the day just for a picnic in the open to the public orchards.

10. One more food-related trip is a **dairy**.

11. That moves us onto animal **breeders** and **pet stores**.

12. After you have exhausted all the cages of hamsters, para-keets, iguanas, and kittens and listened to pleas for one of each, head over to the local **animal shelter**. Compassion can be strengthened there as well as a deeper understanding of the responsibility of pet ownership.

13. We have visited two **fish hatcheries**. One is the ending of the remarkable journey the salmon make to jump upstream and steps to spawn in the same place they were born. The other was a commercial operation growing sturgeon that I mentioned eralier.

14. Most of us have some childhood memory of a **circus**. Many discussions, as well as ambitious acrobatic feats, may be the result.

15. Young children should have time and room to run and play and so if you are not in the country **parks** should be a staple. Many areas have **water parks** now too, to tempt the little ones outside even in the heat of summer. We spent a year when my kids were little trying to visit every **trail** and park in our town.

16. A trip to see the **outdoor art** in your area can introduce an appreciation for the completion of an idea and give reference to how visual objects and murals portray ideas to a population.

17. **Theaters** often have matinees that are appropriate for young children.

18. While the theater is a type of storytelling, keep your eye on the community calendars for **true storytellers**. An often loved story retold by a master storyteller is likely to inspire and add animation to your conversations.

19. Many large **home improvement stores** offer monthly building workshops for young children. While you're there, take the time to walk the aisles and ask your child to tell you what things are for and then answer his questions.

20. **Hiking.** You can travel the country looking for hikes or hike in your backyard. Hikes introduce many environments and landscapes. A hiker is one who has found some balance in the day if not in life.

21. Because a **fire station tour** is a staple of the 8-11-year-old cub scout program, fire stations are well versed in giving tours. If you're lucky, they'll even invite you back to drop egg contraptions from their truck.

22. **Train stations** are fascinating places for young children. It's fun to watch the bustle of people getting on and off, everyone with a destination, and an unknown story to tell. Not to mention the large trains with all of the different cars. If you don't have a station, you could also have a picnic a safe distance from some tracks to watch the trains as they pass.

23. Little children at a **nursing home** can bring delight to those living there. It also introduces the needs of others to children and can lead to great conversations and respect for others.

24. **University museums** and **collections**. We may not think of taking our littlest ones to a University, but many have a lot of things of interest. One of our local universities has a small portable classrooms filled with trays and trays of insects and students to tell you about them. Another one had an exhibit of carved and painted birds, and another had student portraits in many media lining the walls. Call your local university and ask them about all of the museums, collections and exhibits going on. You are sure to get several that would be interesting to your little ones.

13

WHERE DO I TAKE MY TEENS?

"We must go beyond textbooks, go out into the
bypaths and untrodden depths of the wilderness
and travel and explore and tell the world the
glories of your journey."
John Hope Franklin

I have a toddler who wobbles and falls, and she has the bruises to show for it. But we keep encouraging her. Our teens need room to wobble and occasionally fall too. He needs to learn to stand in a larger world and become comfortable with it. He needs to see the world as his. He should be allowed to wander, explore, discover and delight in all the possibilities and the richness that this world has to offer. And as he does this he will gain an education that moves him to find his place in the world and his relationship to it and to the other people that live and work in it.

As students go on field trips and meet different people, they can imagine events from different points of view. We teach them right and wrong and good and bad as they grow, but when they go out they see that there is also a lot of gray. Do differences in hairstyles matter? What about piercings, tattoos, and shredding of the earlobes? What resources should be available for various groups of people? What is fair in our world and what isn't and who is trying to do things about it? Young children are ready to see these things as black and white, but as they grow they begin to see things as choices people make and that the people themselves are more important. They expand their cultural understanding and empathy for people and societies that do things differently than themselves.

HERE ARE A YEAR'S WORTH OF EXCURSIONS THAT WILL HELP TEENS stretch and grow.

1. FIELD TRIPS CAN BE A CHANCE TO HELP TEENS TAKE THE RISKS THEY desire in a safe way. **Motor boating** is one of the best of these. Before they are allowed on the boats make them learn the safety rules, then within those rules let them try things: water skiing, diving into freezing water and even driving the boat under supervision.

2. **Smaller watercraft** such as **kayaks, canoes,** and **rafts** give a very different experience than the motor boats. We have taken kids in several canoes down a river giving them room to maneuver and put in the hard work themselves, but also staying close enough to keep them safe.

3. Another activity to stretch the teens are **ropes courses** which are often **team building exercises** disguised as high adventure. Look for **zip-lines** as well.

4. **Rock climbing** can be done indoor or out. It is sufficiently treacherous that most youth will be apt to pay attention to the

reason for the rules. And while we want to encourage our kids to do all sorts of things, the fences give us freedom. If you can't go rock climbing a similar experience is **spelunking**. I still remember when I was a teen, our youth group went spelunking off a bridge as we learned about the need to support each other.

5. Teens should gain exposure to multiple sides of an issue. You can have them guess legal consequences of **graffiti**, show them graffiti in town and then visit a **lawyer** to explain in person. At home have students view examples of graffiti as American art and have them take a side and explain their viewpoint using concrete examples.

6. Take them out to feed the **homeless**, and to visit any **tent cities** or areas with a high homeless population. Talk to the people. They are not just service projects; they are individual human beings with individual life stories to share.

7. Volunteer in a **soup kitchen**.

8. Attend a **civil court case** or if your children want to learn more attend a **criminal one**, but be there for the discussions.

9. Visit a **county jail**. One of ours gives tours, but if it doesn't you can still visit the guest areas and get a glimpse of the life there.

10. Attend **town hall meetings** or if possible Senate and House of Representative sessions in your **capitol**.

11. Participate in a **political campaign** or **rally**. Help them not to get swept away with the excitement of it, but to research and think through which side of an issue they fall on. Help them to see other viewpoints and unintended consequences. We want thinking voters and political activists who are intentional and hold values and not those that just get swept up with causes.

12. As they learn about the political processes and their country, they should also learn about their military. Take a tour of a **military base**.

13. Visit **memorials** and **museums** commemorating the wars. Let them see the reasons and the cost.

14. Help them to find the influencers. Take them on a tour of a **newspaper company, television station, radio station** and **publishing houses.**

15. Also bring them to online places they know. Do you have an **Amazon warehouse** nearby? **Facebook headquarters? Apple offices?** The **Apple stores** often have kids classes and camps. I know one family who met many of their favorite Youtubers at a **Youtube conference. Blogging conferences** also abound.

16. Our **water treatment center** doesn't allow anyone under sixteen. If yours is the same, the later high school years are the time to go.

17. Extend the **hiking.** As I write this, my two oldest sons are **backpacking** around a lake in the mountains on an overnight trip with friends and adults.

18. **Long distance bike rides** can give you a chance to look more closely at the habitats, the litter, the weather, while being able to customize your child's challenge. My seventeen year old just came back from a 300-mile bike trip down the coast of California and gained a lot of confidence from doing so.

19. As they move out into the world, they need to think about money too. A trip to the **bank** to open up accounts, get debit cards and talk to the bankers about the service and strategies for saving and borrowing is a necessity.

20. Take your students on formal **university tours** and also tour the **libraries.** Get a calendar and attend an open lecture.

21. A fun trip is one where the teens paint a **guided picture** in one sitting. We have local venues for this, and our art museum has special events. Check both. Also, see if you can find an **artist studio** and talk to the artist about what he does.

22. Get them out to the **art museums,** but look for other museums and revisit several that they did when they were younger.

23. Of course, this is the time to open up the **career opportuni-**

ties in the world even further. Find **factories** and learn about the different jobs. Also look for **small artisan shops, welding companies**, and **photography studios** to learn about the tools, skills, and education they needed to do those jobs. Don't just take them to places they may be interested in working. A well-rounded person has an appreciation for the people who work in a variety of fields and some general knowledge of what they do.

24. If your child hasn't seen a **Broadway play** or **musical**, it's time.

14

WHAT ABOUT MY LARGE FAMILY?

"Field trips have educated, excited and informed our family. They have led us down paths of knowledge and understanding of our world, our history and ourselves." Teri J. Brown

IN A LARGE FAMILY, WE NEED TO FIND TRIPS THAT ARE SUITED TO ALL age ranges. The good news is that most of them can work for everyone. Young children may enjoy more hands on follow up activities, while older children are ready to put what they've learned into words. By verbally engaging older children with thought provoking questions we help them to engage multiple areas of their brain as they have to take into account what they saw and experienced, what they understood before, how they feel about it and what it means to them now.

This is why a field trip to the transfer station works for younger children who may understand that this is where my garbage goes. But it also works for older students who learn that

Idaho has a garbage pile as large as a mountain, and the reality of that sinks in on an emotional level as they stare at the much smaller piles at the local transfer station.

Younger children may be more interested in the here and now and the older in the human aspects and connections between all of the places you go.

1. Take the kids to **large** and **unique farms**. If possible visit an **organic** and a **non-organic farm**. The younger children will learn about where their food comes from while the older children can begin to participate in the many food debates in our country.

2. As you are traveling, take the **neighborhood routes**. It helps everyone to have more than just a literary perspective of **richer** and **poorer neighborhoods, country homes** and **city apartments**.

3. Involve them in a **community effort**. Justserve.org has opportunities by zip code. Give your children the power to feel they can do something about a problem they are seeing. We've worked with our **historical society** to lay a brick walk. We've also helped gather supplies for refugees and done several **fundraisers**.

4. Teach the kids about money, bartering, and bargains and head to several **yard sales**. A lot of economic lessons are learned by giving them a few dollars and a goal.

5. Tours of **caves**, especially with some understanding of the pre-World War 2 public works projects.

6. **Student plays, professional plays** and **semi-professional**.

7. **Roller skating** and **ice skating**.

8. Don't be intimidated by all the kids and work to **camp** with a large family. It is worth it. We have found that going with other families is very helpful. Split the responsibilities, but keep it simple. I'm known to have cereal for breakfast, sandwiches for lunch and hotdogs for dinner. Nothing too complex. The point is to enjoy the outdoors. Let the little ones get dirty, go on **hikes** and play.

9. One of the best places to camp or go on day trips to are the

State and **National Parks.** We learned about the **Junior Ranger program** a couple of years ago, so for those as behind the curve as we are here is a link to the Junior Ranger Programs. https://www.nps.gov/kids/jrRangers.cfm

10. Head to a **post office** for a tour and have each child bring a postcard or letter to mail to someone.

11. A **food processing plant** is an easy place to follow up with different levels of understanding. The younger children can learn one of the steps between the **farm** and **the grocery store.** The middle children can focus on the processes and operations of the machines, and the older children can look for areas where food contamination could occur and what the plant does to prevent it.

12. **Museums** again, but look especially for hands-on museums with many exhibits.

13. Take a tour of the **state capitol.**

14. Children can study the processes needed in manufacturing raw materials by visiting a **textile factory,** a **lumber mill** or a **grain mill.** They can learn how these things used to be processed and compare how things are different or the same now. You can also visit **artisans** who process **wool,** and **wood** by hand to compare the difference between the two.

15. We have had a **veterinary office** give us a very good tour and tips for the kids who care for the animals.

16. When it's fair time head out to the **county** or **state fair,** which always has lots to see. We also have an heirloom food fair, and fairs specializing in garlic, tulips, and other produce.

17. Children should be able to look at their houses and know where they get most of the things there including power and water. Seek out tours with **power plants** and **water districts.**

18. **Conservation groups** lead activities about methods to conserve all our resources. We have a **free small museum** with **hands-on exhibits** and a **water conservation park** with hands-on tips and the best plants for the area.

19. In addition to learning about the things that come into our houses, we should learn about what goes out. If you have a **sewage treatment center,** take a tour.

20. A **transfer station** is where garbage is taken after being picked up and before being sorted for the **dump** or **recycling centers.** After we took our children and learned how much of our garbage had to be sorted by hand, we all became much more careful to sort our garbage into the right can.

21. Weather is a subject that spans the ages. See if you can, visit a **weather station** or have a **meteorologist** talk with your family or group.

22. **Large aquariums** have a lot to offer as children learn about fish, ecosystems and interactions between the ocean species but also those on land and in the ocean.

23. If you live in an area with **mines** or **quarries,** these can be quite interesting as they are so rich with history.

24. **Living history museums** and **reenactments** have places you can step aside if you need to nurse a baby, but also have a lot going on to learn from and to see.

15

I HAVE A CHILD WITH SPECIAL NEEDS

"Learning is a lifelong endeavor, and it can take place anywhere and at anytime." Peter Chause

EACH OR OUR CHILDREN ARE SO DIFFERENT FROM EACH OTHER, AND that holds true for each child with special needs. I can't address every situation but look through the ideas below and all of the others in this book to find ones that will work best for your child. But don't hesitate to stretch. If there aren't any safety concerns, keep going, keep trying.

As a special needs parent, we learn to be an advocate for our children and to be in tune to their needs, which is not the same things as controlling the student and the situation. But we know what to look for and what may be obstacles. If our child can't read then, a site with a lot of plaques won't be fun without someone to read them or a verbal tour led by a guide who already knows what all those signs have to say. In the same way, we need to advocate in our excursions. Let guides know, help the site to be aware of your needs. We can call ahead, and get special help. Enlist a relative or friend if you need another set of hands. Keep using the stroller if it's appropriate. Some children are crowd averse; others may not be able to walk for a long time or need a smooth surface. Each of these will present different needs, so check ahead and think of your particular child to see if it is appropriate. Many popular sites have specific accommodations and information on their websites.

When getting ready for a field trip, we need to remember that if a student gets embarrassed or frustrated, they will likely not be able to stay in a state where they can concentrate and learn. To help them we should explicitly teach the behavioral expectations, from when it's appropriate to ask a question to how we can diffuse a situation if someone else acts inappropriately. This includes what to say when people point or say something to the child. I know we want to protect our kids from these comments, but they need to be given the power that comes with knowing how to deal with them. It does no good to get offended. Instead, try explaining that people are naturally curious and they are especially curious about other people. People will look and can be greeted with a smile or a wave. Practice what you will say ahead of time. I've been asked by strangers if they can take a picture of my child who has dwarfism. I have no qualms telling the well-meaning grandma or the young father, "no, that's not appropriate." Let your child know that if a situation gets too hard, you'll be right there. While they are learning how to interact with the world, you'll protect them and not let things get too much, and you'll guide and empower them to do it too.

If you have anxious children, you might want to provide them with a map of the site, with exits and bathrooms marked. If a student is concerned about their basic needs and safety they can't concentrate on higher level learning. For very anxious children show them photos and exhibits found online to help them feel familiar with the environment when they arrive. This is also a good reason to go more than once. The child can become familiar with a place which leaves more room for learning. Balance the novel with the familiar; you know your child. As they continue going to new places, the newness will become less scary. Also as you begin building adventures into your routines, your children will be able to understand the expectations and learn what to do.

Before you go, when you get there, and throughout the trip, check to see if the student's needs anything physically, emotionally or developmentally.

Take from the ideas below what you can, switch them out for other trips, but here are 24 I hope you can use as a good starting place.

1. Look for outdoor art. Check your city websites and go on an **outdoor sculpture tour.**

2. **Historical markers** are also a great outdoor learning point. What can you learn about your city from stopping at the **landmarks** and **plaques**? What about other cities on your way? Maybe you have wiggly kids, and who doesn't? When you are traveling taking frequent historical marker breaks, or landmark breaks can break up a trip and add value.

3. Along the same avenue we can look for **driving tours.** I wish there was a website that focused on CD's that you could purchase all over for audio tours. The closest I can find is travelaudios.com which focuses on several major National Parks. Learnoutloud.com is another one that has gathered several sources. There are a lot more, but you need to search for audio tours in locations near you or that you are willing to travel.

4. While we are still driving we need to find all of those **scenic stopping places.** Let's take pictures and have picnics at all of the

places suggested by the road signs and let's stop at the scenic lookout.

5. Another way to get out and about and learn about terrains, map skills and communication is to go **geocaching**. Geocaching is like a treasure hunt using a GPS system. Go to geocaching.com and type in your area to find caches near you. Bring a notebook to collect stamps and trinkets to trade for other trinkets in the box if you want. **Letterboxing** is similar but uses clues instead of GPS coordinates. You can find information at www.letterboxing.org.

6. Teach your children how to get **bus** tickets and how to ride the bus, transfer to **light rails** and get to where they want to go. We took a large group from our individual neighborhoods, either meeting each other as the bus picked us up on our various routes or at the local college where the main bus hub was located. We then took the bus into the city to see a sports arena being built and have lunch at the mall. Did I mention it was raining? Nothing like teaching problem solving on your feet and an adventurous, you-can't-stop-me attitude.

7. Visit **old towns**. **Ghost towns** can be fun, while giving the kids a realistic view of television. We saw a show on a haunted house in a town with a population of 70 people. We visited the town and talked to the store owners. The ice cream shop/diner owner let us know the scariest thing in town was the city council meetings when everyone couldn't get along. The junk shop owner just smiled and asked if we'd been watching Youtube. You mean, Youtube has made up videos? There are so many things to see in a historic town. A walk through them and a peek in at a store is well worth the look at the different lifestyles offered.

8. **Public gardens** make beautiful spots to learn about native and exotic plants. We have a school near us that is known for its agricultural studies that has a great garden, and an **arboretum**. Look for **public vegetable gardens, rose gardens** and **other outdoor spaces** with plant themes.

9. Most **bowling alleys** have bumpers and ramps to help those who need it to bowl and can be a fun activity for everyone to participate in.

10. **Craft fairs** can lead to many inspired afternoons and a possibility of making money on the side. When I was a child my mom let us participate in craft fairs she sold at, and we learned what sold and the amount of time it takes to produce all of the handmade products.

11. Head out on a **tour** to your local **ice cream**, **beverage** or **candy company**. Many of these offer free samples after, yum.

12. Along the same line, **tour fast food** and **restaurant chains**. Come with questions.

13. Not only does the Washington DC Red Cross have regular tours featuring their beautiful Tiffany Windows, your local **Red Cross** may do tours as well.

14. Second hand chains such as, **Goodwill, Deseret Industries** and **The Salvation Army** can provide tours and a chance to ask questions about training programs for those that may need help with independent living skills and support.

15. **Neighborhood safety walks** can be an important outing. We have a model of a town that is children sized with tours around the town that teach about all aspects of safety, including crosswalks, fire, "yell & tell," traffic, tricky people, railroad crossing, garbage trucks, biking and skateboard, and for older kids driving defense and workplace safety. You can use neighborhood walks to teach each of these concepts too or work with a group having each adult teach a different part somewhere in the city.

16. **Pools** can be scary places for some kids, which is one reason they need to learn how to be safe near them. Learning how to swim is an important life skill for everyone and can help you feel more comfortable heading to lakes, rivers and oceans.

17. Book a formal tour of the **library** to help the kids discover all of the opportunities available to them.

18. Head out to a **movie** adaptation of a book, or other educational movie. If you need to train behavior go to an early viewing when the theaters aren't crowded or head to a summer $1 movie if your local theater participates. These are usually not quiet and many people are juggling babies and an occasional toddler runs down the aisle chased by a parent trying to duck and appear smaller. The other adults in the room only smile, and remember the summer they were training their little one, now sitting riveted in the chair next to them.

19. **Home tours** allow a glimpse into how someone else may live. I know I'm weird but my children and I have been found touring **model homes** just for fun, but other homes offer tours, **historical homes, celebrity homes, assisted living** and other places people live or have lived.

20. Visit an **archeology dig site**, watch people at work and in some cases participate yourself. You can also recreate such an experience by burying items in the sand and when they are unearthed asking what it might tell us about the people who used them.

21. Bring in **experts to you.** This can be informal, inviting people to dinner and asking them about their hobbies and jobs. You can also ask people to come share in a more formal way. We had a glass artist come and teach the kids how to make jewelry, she set out pieces of glass and let them design a necklace or pin while she taught about the types of glass and the history of working with it. She then took it back to her studio to melt it together. We also invited in a cake decorator for two sessions to teach the kids and their friends how to decorate cakes. By having the learning experiences come to you, you can control the environment and decrease the anxiety kids might feel.

22. Check the events calendar of **large buildings** in your area. Many types of **conventions** are open to the public and make perfect places to visit. Our calendar currently has things such as a

gem and rock shows, Greek festival, reptile show, stamp and scrap-
book show, arts festival, and naturalization ceremonies.

23. A great service project to teach responsibility and ownership is **picking up trash**. Teach safety-don't pick up sharp items or
needles, use gloves or grabbing devices. There is pride in knowing
you have contributed.

24. You can lay out a blanket and watch **air shows** or **hot air
balloon events**. Some cities even have **kite flying** events. While
you're looking up **watch the clouds** and learn to identify them and
predict what will happen next.

16

WE NEED TO GO ON NIGHTS AND WEEKENDS

"One exciting aspect of taking trips is that neither the teacher nor the children can predict all the particulars of their experience- there are surprises." Salvatore Vascellaro

H omeschoolers come in all shapes and sizes, even ones with parents who work during the day and homeschool in the evening and on weekends. They will need to take their field trips then too. Other families don't feel comfortable going on excursions without both parents or other adults who might work during the day. Still, others may only have one car. There are still trips you can go on. In fact, many of the ones mentioned in earlier chapters are available to you, but here are a years worth of trips that may be especially relevant.

1. MOVIE THEATERS ARE AN EASY TRIP. IN ORDER TO KEEP IT MORE educational, look for the educational documentaries in the **Imax theaters**. Be sure to check for the teacher discount programs.

2. If you are lucky enough to still have a **drive-in theater**, night is the only time you will be able to catch a show. Our drive-in movie theater also becomes a **farmer's market** on Saturday mornings.

3. Major and minor league **sporting events** often happen during the evening and weekends to draw a crowd.

4. Look for **large** and **small concerts**. Our art museum hires semi-professionals to do periodic performances.

5. Return to your venue calendar and look for **symphonies, plays, operas** and **ballets**, which are also usually at night.

6. Our city has **visiting authors, comedians**, and **TV personalities** come and give inspirational lectures six times a year. You have to buy the whole thing as a package but what a great way to study speech along with the topics which are presented. Look at college and universities for **lectures** in the evening as well.

7. Look at the **small town calendars** as well. We have **comedians in the parks, concerts in the park, celebrations** and **food truck nights**.

8. Food makes a good introduction to different cultures. Look for different **ethnic restaurants** to visit as a family and try native dishes to that culture.

9. In some locations, you can have your dinner on an **evening boat cruise** as an introduction to the ocean and to see the sunset.

10. The **sunset** can make a really solid unit study. Try viewing it from many locations. Learn why it looks the way it looks and how clean air versus pollution has an effect on it.

11. If you have a **bird sanctuary** and visit at sunset you can see the birds who spend their days on the water head to the field for the night and the ones who spend their days in the fields soar in and land on the water for the evening.

12. Various **evening or night hikes** can have a different feel than during the day. You may see animals coming out as many are more active at dusk. You can also do a **listening hike,** or just find a

spot without the noise of traffic to **sit and listen to the sounds of nature.**

13. If you have a **migration path** near you, head to watch the birds, butterflies or large mammals as they move. Take pictures.

14. In addition to watching the birds go in to roost, you can see the **bats and owls** come out at night. Our **nature preserve** even has special evenings where they do **bat sightings.**

15. A **photography scavenger hunt** can be done at any time of day, outside or in. Make sure each person has a way of taking photos. You can look for various things around your city or in the woods, take photos and then compare what everyone got.

16. **Malls** stay open late and have a lot to teach. They often have **bookstores, curiosity shops, pet stores**, and **Lego stores.** Ours has an **Apple store** with classes as well. Talk to shop owners, look at products. Learn about the running of a store, and a mall along with what is actually in it.

17. If it's dark out, but you still want to see some plants head to a **nursery or garden shop.** The people who work there are often experts at identifying plants and knowing how to care for each properly. You can make it a project to learn the name and needs of every plant on your property or street.

18. Head to a **town hall meeting** to learn about the needs and issues surrounding your town. There will be a lot to talk about after and your children may even want to get involved with an issue.

19. Our **historical society** also meets in the evening, and there are many very enthusiastic people, who would welcome new faces. I attended a **pioneer society** with my mom when I was in high school and learned to love the many older ladies and all their stories.

20. **Hospitals** often have visiting times in the evening and can be a great place to help your children get to know and become comfortable with those in different circumstances than your own.

Hospitals may also offer tours, and not just the ones for expectant mothers.

21. **Auctions** often happen at night. For a long time, we had a furniture and household goods auction that was held every Friday night. If you live near a **port**, you may be able to watch as the ships come in with food to sell to the various buyers representing restaurants and grocery stores.

22. **Astronomy trips** can only be done at night. Many universities have large telescopes with nights open to the public.

23. My husband takes the kids **stargazing** every August. He lays out blankets on the soccer field in the park near our house and tells them if they are not quiet or if they get off of their blanket the August park monster will come and get them. Then he points out stars and constellations, and they watch for falling stars until inevitably someone starts to get restless. Games of tag and tickles ensue until they are ready to come home tired out and ready to flop into bed.

24. Look for **meet-ups** and **clubs** that meet in the evenings and weekends. You can often attend once for free. In our area we have stroller clubs, various sports, writing, mastermind groups, finances, and teen events-such as skateboarding, brainstorming, and dances.

WHERE TO GO CLOSE TO HOME FOR CHEAP OR FREE

"To truly know the world, look deep within your own being. To truly know yourself, take a real interest in the world." Rudolf Steiner

*I*f you flipped to this chapter first, make sure you skim through all of the other chapters in this section, as all of them include more ideas that are also free.

You do not need to spend a lot or anything at all to give your children an awesome education. In the way of field trips here are enough to go on two a month for a year and most can often be found quite close to home or your nearest mid-sized town.

1. PRINT OUT A MAP, CONTOUR IF POSSIBLE, OF YOUR TOWN OR AREA. Take a trip with your map in hand and head to any **waterways**, **major streets** and **parks**. Mark them on your map. When you come home, hang up the map and mark all new excursions to keep a record of how many parts of your town you've visited.

2. Do the same things as above but with a **parks** and rec map of all the **trails** and parks. We spent one year trying to hit every trail in our town-they just built more.

3. Visit a **children's court**. These are open to the public and give kids a great sense of the judicial system.

4. **Town hall meetings**, show kids that the average Joe really does have a voice.

5. If you have especially brave children or one brave friend, get out and **interview people** you see on camera. My daughter and a friend asked people what they thought about homeschooling and then compared it to what really happens and made a short film.

6. Go **data collecting**. Put a scientific or sociology question to the test and then take the kids to observe. I got a lot of comments on my family size when I was younger and had my many children in tow. I remember once recording how many negative versus positive comments I got for a couple weeks and I wrote a paper on it for a class I was in. You could also make predictions, observe and write or graph about how many of a certain color car go by, how many couples visit the mall vs. singles, what time of day is the dog park most popular and how many people order ice cream at a local store in different temperature increments.

7. A **body of water** makes a great trip, to search for **erosion**. You can also follow a river or stream on foot, bike or car and stop to examine it periodically until is reaches a larger body of water.

8. **Police station tours.**

9. Teach your children how to comparison shop. Choose ten things you regularly buy and then visit **five stores** and record how much the items are in each store.

10. Head to an **antique store** and talk about how different things were used and what we would do the same thing with today.

11. Even if **car shows** are not your thing, you should take the

kids at least once just to see the light sparkle in the owner's eyes when they talk about their cars.

12. **Small local shops.** An owner of a niche local shop got into it because she loves it. Usually that means you can convince her to tell you about it. Look for **coin shops, stamp shops, music stores** and **art stands.**

13. **Murals.** I didn't think we had any in our town, though I knew the city one over does. I was wrong. Look for them, study why they were made, what it means about the maker and what it means about the person who commissioned it. Then if you are a hands on type make one of your own to hang on your back fence, at least until it rains.

14. Keep tabs on any **bookstores** around for **author readings or signings.** Come with questions, too.

15. While you're at it go to **poetry readings** at the bookstores or other presentations. Quiz the owner of the store on the top selling books and get his opinion as to why. He's not working there because he hates books.

16. Volunteer at the **food bank** or **Meals on Wheels** for a few hours.

17. Walk through **historic towns** and look at the **architecture** of the buildings.

18. Visit and sketch every **bridge** in your area. Have the kids identify what type they are and explain how they think they were made.

19. Go on a **nature walk in the city.** Look for the places nature is poking through in the cracks and holes.

20. **Pet stores.** We even have different ones dedicated to reptiles, birds and fish.

21. Ask for a tour of an **eye doctor office. Dental** and **chiro-practic offices** may also be willing to give your kids a tour and teach them about what they do.

22. Look for a **print shop.** These are fascinating places to see

how something can be taken from an idea all the way to completed project.

23. Look for tours or chances to walk through other **churches**, **temples** or **cathedrals**. Look at architecture and learn a little about the religion and the people who use the building.

24. **Cemeteries** are intriguing places to learn about the history of an area and the families that live there. They give a perspective on life and can show a clever turn of phrase that naturally leads to a writing project.

18

OTHER IDEAS

"What children need is not new and better curricula but access to more and more of the real world ...to make it easier for them to get where they want to go and to find out what they want to find out." John Holt

WE'VE TALKED ABOUT WHERE TO LOOK FOR IDEAS. I'VE GIVEN YOU over 150 ideas in the previous scenarios. I encourage you as you look for ideas to make sure you read through those chapters even if the circumstance doesn't apply to you. Just because a trip is great for a large family or a teen does not mean it is not great for you.

Here are a few more ideas to go on and to get you thinking. But before you look at this list, look up every museum and community calendar in your town, nearby towns, universities and everywhere previously mentioned.

1. DESERTS

2. Beaches
3. Islands
4. Mountains
5. Volcanoes
6. Geologic formations
7. River Walks
8. Waterfalls
9. Dams
10. Cliffs, cliff dwelling homes
11. Rodeos
12. Windmills
13. Lighthouses
14. Skyscrapers
15. Nuclear Power Plants
16. Models
17. Sports arenas
18. One room schoolhouses
19. Historic Forts
20. Missions
21. Gold panning/natural resource gathering
22. Miniature golf
23. Skiing
24. Snowshoes
25. Snow
26. Canoe, raft, kayak
27. Run a 5k
28. Pedal boats
29. Archery ranges
30. Talent shows
31. Children's music recitals
32. Tea parties
33. Car dealerships
34. Tours of military boats, planes and rockets

35. Car races
36. Horse races
37. Animal training facilities
38. Native animal enclosures
39. Birdwatching
40. Falcon flying
41. Animal auctions
42. Butcher
43. Other types of auctions
44. Craft class
45. One time cooking class
46. One time gardening class
47. Chess/game days competitions
48. Spelling Bees
49. Magic shows/shops
50. Literary sites
51. Estates/manors/plantations
52. Historical archives
53. Family history centers
54. Cultural stores
55. Japanese Gardens
56. Halls/sidewalks of fame
57. Beekeepers
58. Independent films and small viewings
59. Flea Markets
60. Farm to Fork Dinners
61. Maker Fairs
62. Maker/hacker Labs
63. Co-working spaces

19

MAKING MEMORIES

"Homeschooling allows you the freedom to step off the highway of learning and take a more scenic route along a dirt road."
Tamara L. Chilver

I don't know all of the goals you have for raising your children. I have yet to perfectly articulate the goals I have for raising mine, but I know field trips are helping me with many of them. They are also helping me to enjoy the time I get to have them in my house.

I've also found the field trips help with many skills I see emerging in my children. They are developing more bravery and confidence as they build so many relationships with the world and really feel like they belong to it. They are confident as they get out and talk to so many people and realize others listen to them and want to share. They are empowered to know their ideas can be heard and questions can be asked. They learn respect as we go to so many places and they have to understand how to act and what is appropriate in each setting. They also learn to respect all types of businesses and workers as they see the interconnectedness and complexity of what everyone does to build a community. They develop their curiosity as they see so many things they have never heard, never read about and never seen. They are also able to feel like they can discover what they are curious about since there is often a place or person they can find the answers from. They are humble and rarely think they know it all as they are introduced to new places and ideas regularly and realize that each of these places have years of study and work behind them. The humility and curiosity help them to be teachable.

Some children who have turned off in the public school after years of being in an environment that doesn't fit them can be brought back to learning by field trips that spark the imagination and by seeing there are so many things to learn and so many ways to learn them.

As field trips bond the traveling companions, the families and groups grow closer together. They develop a common understanding of subjects and the community that they can pull from in their descriptions and discussion. They understand that while the world is a beautiful and wonderful place it is the relationships with others that are most important. Field trips help students to increase their knowledge base and develop a very broad understanding. Some people travel the world to gain a better understanding of humanity and our interactions with it, and that would be the ultimate field trip, but even intense explorations of your own region of the world can introduce so many topics and types of people and how they express themselves and how they have figured out what space in the world they want to occupy that a broad understanding of it can be achieved without venturing more than two hours from home.

Field trips help type A people to be more spontaneous as we see something that would be great to add to our learning and then we just get up and go do it. They help the fun loving, fly-by-the-seat-of-your-pants type people to know that in many cases field trips need to be planned. They help the introvert get out and see things, and they help the extrovert to let others shine as they learn to listen attentively.

Most future professions will also be benefited by field trips. Think of an architect who has visited a variety of buildings, a landscape designer who has walked through public gardens, university campuses and run-down parts of towns. It will help someone who has to give presentations when they look back and remember what made the guides effective and the presentations work. It will help someone who writes, and exchanges ideas, have much to contribute.

Because of all the benefits of field trips, it's important that we don't stop taking them in elementary—they may be even more important as the student gets older. During the middle school and high school years, it helps for them to see the world outside of themselves. They are changing and need to be opening to the world even more. They need authentic experiences with it. They need to see some of the real problems and meet some of the real problem solvers. They need to explore the world around them as they are finding their place in it.

Well, planned field trips will also allow students to see how the books they are reading and how other things they are learning can be applied to the real world. The connections begin to be evident. Unless they aren't. Then the students see a variety of things and begin to meet so many people they begin to see that the skills they are learning in their other studies will be applied somewhere even if they don't see where right now.

These trips will enliven the discussions your children are able to have, help them to relate to others and make them better conversationalists as they have experiences in many topics to draw on when talking to new people.

Take joy in your children, remember that homeschooling isn't just about preparing them for the future but it's about having fun with them right now. As we get out into the world we also want to make sure we leave lots of downtime. Have variety but not overwhelmed busy, leave time for reflection. When kids start to incorporate what they are learning in their play you know you have the right amount of feeding their imagination and the right amount of free time.

We went to see Jim Weiss the storyteller. While it was geared to 4th grade and up, I took all of mine and figured the youngers would get what they get and I'd take them out if needed, which I did at one point, because my daughter kept standing up and leaning on the stage as he was speaking. She'd remember for a minute but then as he'd talk she'd start to lean forward fascinated.

During the workshop he had given advice on public speaking and how not to be scared. Later when she was playing I could hear her say "when you are talking, look out at peoples' eyebrows, they will think you are looking at their eyes." She's five and she may not have picked up everything but she picked up a nugget. And by allowing her time to play too, she's able to cement those nuggets and incorporate them into her world.

Other ways of learning can be beautiful and wonderful, but we have freedom, not available to many, and we have a wonderful world to see and participate in it. Let's do it. Let's get out there and see everything that we can.

I'd love to hear about your adventures or if you have any questions. Please email me at livelearnworkathome@gmail.com and come visit me at www.livelearnworkathome.com.

ndnotes

A Different Way to Learn

1. Leah Melber *"Informal Learning and Field Trips: Engaging Stidents in Standards-Based Experiences Across the k-5 Curriculum."* *Corwin Press, 2007, pg. 119*

Learning in the Real World

1. Salvatore Vascellaro *"Out of the Classroom and Into the World: Learning from Field Trips, Educating from Experience and Unlocking the Potential of our Students and Our Teachers."* The New Press, 2011, pg. 5

2. Joy Hakim War, Peace and All that Jazz, Book 9 of A History of US Series. Oxford University Press, 2002.

3. The Jump$tart Coalation. "Jump$Tart's Reality Check." *Jumpstart.org, The Jump$Tart Coalation, Jan. 2017, www.jump-start.org/reality-check.html.*

The Research

1. John Holt What Do I Do Monday? Heinemann, 1995.

2. Jennifer DeWitt & Martin Storksdieck *"A Short Review of*

School Field Trip: Key Findings from the Past and Implications for the Future." Visitor Studies, Volume 11, Issue 2, 2008.

3. Joy Telu, Hamilton Ekeke "Relative Effectiveness of Expository and Field Trip Methods of Teaching on Students' Achievement in Ecology." International Journal of Science Education, Volume 29, Issue 15, 2007.

4. Jay P Green, Brian Kisida et al "The Educational Value of Field Trips Taking Students to an Art Museum Improves Critical Thinking SKills, and More." Education Next, Winter 2014.

5. Avi Hofstein, Nir Orion "Factors that influence learning during a scientific field trip in a natural environment," JRST, Volume 31, Issue 10, December 1994.

6. John H. Falk, John D. Balling "The Field Trip Milieu: Learning and Behavior as a Function of Contextual Events" The Journal of Educational Research, Volume 76, Issue 1982 1982.

7. W. Wade Martin, John H. Falk, John D. Balling, "Environmental Effects on Learning: The Outdoor Field Trip" Science Journal, Volume 65, Issue 3 July 1981.

8. Leah Melber Informal Learning and Field Trips;Engaging Students in Standards-Based Experiences across the K-5 Curriculum, Skyhorse Publishing, 2014.

9. Teri J. Brown Day Tripping, Champion Press LTD. 2003.

10. Kathleen Carroll A Guide to Great Field Trips Zephyr Press 2007.

11. Kwok Chan Lai "Freedom to Learn: A study of the Experiences of Secondary School Teachers and Students in Geography Field Trip" International Research in Geographical and Environmental Education, Volume 8, Issue 3, 1999.

12. Kelli Becton "The Value of Travel for Homeschooling" Adventure Homeschool: Hands on Learning, http://adventurehomeschool.com/2015/04/03/the-value-of-travel-for-homeschooling/ April 3, 2015.

13. John H. Falk, W. Wade Martin, John D. Balling "The Novel Field-Trip Phenomenon: Adjustment to Novel Setting Interferes with

Task Learning," *Journal of Research in Science Teaching, Volume 15, Issue 2, March 1978.*

14. Angela Richter, *"Taking Your Children to Educational Places" Together with Family, http://togetherwithfamily.com/taking-your-children-to-educational-places/, October 16, 2014.*

15. Amy Moore, *"Five Reasons Why You Should be Taking Your Children to Historical Sites" Family Travel Everything Everywhere, http://familytravel.everything-everywhere.com/2013/07/five-reasons-why-you-should-be-taking-your-children-to-historical-site/ July 3, 2013.*

16. Katrina Schwartz, *"How Field Trips Build Critical Thinking Skills," Mind/Shift October 9, 2013.*

17. John H. Falk, Lynn D. Dierking *"School Field Trips: Assessing Their Long Term Impact," Curator: The Museum Journal Volume 40, Issue 3 September 1997.*

18. Raymond A. Dixon, Ryan A. Brown, *"Transfer of Learning: Connecting Concepts During Problem Solving" Journal of Technology Education, Volume 24, Number 1, Fall 2012.*

19. James Farmer, Doug Knapp & Gregory M. Benton, *"An Elementary School Environmental Education Field Trip: Long-Term Effect on Ecological and Environmental Knowledge and Attitude Development" The Journal of Envirnmental Education Volume 38, Issue 3 2007.*

20. Wendy S. Nielsen, Samson Nshon, David Anderson, *"Metacognitive Engagement During Field-Trip Experiences: A Case Study of Students in an Amusement Park Physics Program," Journal of Research in Science Teaching, Volume 46, Issue 3, March 2009.*

OVERCOMING EXCUSES NOT TO GO

1. G. K. CHESTERTSON, *"THE RIDDLE OF THE IVY," TREMENDOUS Trifles, Methuen, 1909.*

2. Salvatore Vascellaro *"Out of the Classroom and Into the World: Learning from Field Trips, Educating from Experience and Unlocking the Potential of our Students and Our Teachers"* The New Press, 2011.

3. J.D. Novak, & A.J. Canas, *"The Theory Underlying Cocept Maps and How To Construct and Use Them,"* Technical Report IHMC January, 2006.

ARE OUTINGS IMPORTANT IN MY EDUCATIONAL PHILISOHPY?

1. DR. SEUSS, *"OH, THE PLACES YOU'LL GO"* RANDOM HOUSE, JANUARY 22, 1990.

2. Charlotte Mason *"School Education"* pg. 66, K. Paul, Trench, Trubner & Company, 1905.

3. Raymond Moore, Dorothy Moore & Dennis Moore, *"Better Late Than Early: A New Approach to Your Child's Education"* Reader's Digest Association; 1st edition August 1989.

DURING A PERIOD OF DETOX

1. MARIA MONTESSORI, *"THE ABSORBANT MIND,"* HOLT PAPERBACKS; Reprint edition October 15, 1995.

TECHNOLOGY AND FIELD TRIPS

1. ANGELA MAIERS, *"THE PASSION-DRIVEN CLASSROOM"* ROUTLEDGE, September 13, 2017.

2. J.I. Spicer, J. Stratford, *"Student Perceptions of a VIrtual Field*

Trip to Replace a Real Field Trips," *Journal of Computer Assisted Learning*, Volume 17, Issue 4, December 2001, pages 345-354.

3. A.J. Obadiora, *"Comparative Effectiveness of Virtual Field Trip and Real Field Trip on Students' Academic Performance in Social Studies in Osun State Secondary Schools,"* Mediterranean Journal of Social Sciences, Volume 7, Issue 1, January 2016.

4. Kara Wilkins, *"250 Virtual Field Trips...Most of Them are Free,"* To Engage Them All! May 31, 2017.

HOW TO SET UP A FIELD TRIP

1. TONY WHEELER, *"LONELY PLANET"* LONELY PLANET PUBLISHING *Company. 2007.*
http://creativestarlearning.co.uk/c/maths-outdoors/

I HAVE TO REPORT ON OUR LEARNING

1. GEORGE SANTAYANA, *"WHY I AM NOT A MARXIST,"* MODERN *Monthly, Volume 9, April, 1935.*

2. *A2Z Homeschool, "Content Standards-Common Core and Others,"* http://a2zhomeschooling.com/materials/curriculum_shop/content_standards/ , September 17, 2017.

WHERE TO FIND PLACES TO GO

1. CHARLOTTE MASON, *"HOME EDUCATION, VOLUME 1,"* WILDER *Publications, March 2009.*

WHERE CAN I TAKE MY LITTLE ONES?

1. MARIA MONTESSORI, *"THE ABSORBANT MIND,"* HOLT PAPERBACKS; *Reprint edition October 15, 1995.*

WHAT ABOUT MY LARGE FAMILY?

1. TERI J. BROWN, *"DAY TRIPPING,"* CHAMPION PRESS, LTD., 2003.
   I Have a Special Needs Child

1. KATHLEEN CARROLL *A GUIDE TO GREAT FIELD TRIPS* ZEPHYR PRESS 2007.

WE NEED TO GO ON NIGHTS AND WEEKENDS

1. SALVATORE VASCELLARO *"OUT OF THE CLASSROOM AND INTO THE World: Learning from Field Trips, Educating from Experience and Unlocking the Potential of our Students and Our Teachers"* The New Press, 2011.

WHERE TO GO CLOSE TO HOME

1. RUDOLF STEINER "THE CHILDS CHANGING CONSCIOUSNESS AND Waldorf Education" Rodulf Steiner Pr, January 1988.

OTHER IDEAS

1. JOHN HOLT, PAT FARENGA "TEACH YOUR OWN: THE JOHN HOLT Book of Homeschooling" De Capo Press, April 2003.

MAKING MEMORIES

1. TAMARA L. CHILVER "HOW TO TEACH YOUR CHILD: SIMPLE Tools for Homeschool Moms" Createspace Independent Publishing Platform, March 20, 2013.

Made in the USA
Monee, IL
22 July 2020